Together
by Grace

Introducing
the Lutherans

Edited by
Kathryn A. Kleinhans

AUGSBURG FORTRESS

As part of the ELCA's observance of the 500th anniversary of the Reformation, this resource was shaped by a Congregation Reformation Resources task force, convened jointly by the Office of the Presiding Bishop, ELCA, and Augsburg Fortress. Members of the task force were Linda Witte Henke, Kathryn Kleinhans, Craig Mueller, and Carmelo Santos, with staff participation by H. Karl Reko, Marcus Kunz, Heather Dean, Robert Farlee, and Martin A. Seltz. Gratitude is expressed to Thrivent Financial for support through its Reformation Anniversary Grant Program that assisted in the funding of Congregation Reformation Resources development.

General Editor: Kathryn A. Kleinhans
Editor: Robert Farlee
Cover design: Laurie Ingram
Interior design and typesetting: The HK Scriptorium, Inc.

The paper used in this publication meets the minimum requirements of American National Standard for Information Sciences—Permanence of Paper for Printed Materials, ANSI Z329.48-1984.

Manufactured in the U.S.A.

ISBN 978-1-5064-0638-1

25 24 23 22 21 20 19 18 17   6 7 8 9 10

Contents

Contents

Contents

Contents

Editor's Introduction

One doesn't get the opportunity to celebrate 500th anniversaries very often. The year 2017 marks the 500th anniversary of the beginning of the Protestant Reformation. The precise date, October 31, 1517, is associated with Martin Luther's posting of Ninety-Five Theses against the sale of indulgences on the door of the Castle Church in Wittenberg, in the territory then known as Electoral Saxony and now a part of Germany.

This event—and the movement it ignited—had world-changing consequences. This claim isn't just a matter of Lutheran pride. When the calendar turned from 1999 to 2000, many news sources and historians generated lists: the top ten or one hundred people of the millennium, the top ten or one hundred events of the millennium. Martin Luther was on every list, usually in the top five. Luther's posting of the Ninety-Five Theses also ranked highly in the top events lists. Clearly, Luther and what he did 500 years ago had a lasting impact.

As a university professor and as a preacher, Luther's goal was to restore the gospel—the good news of God's grace received as a gift through faith in Jesus Christ crucified and risen for us—to its central place in the life of the church. Luther's *evangelical* (meaning "related to the gospel") reform movement began within the Roman Catholic Church but eventually led to the creation of a separate Christian church body. Five hundred years later, this "Lutheran" branch of Christianity that came about as a result of Luther's teaching and preaching numbers seventy-five million members around the world.

The articles in this book explore the rich and lasting legacy of Martin Luther and the Reformation. This legacy consists not only in the theology Luther articulated or the churches that resulted but also in the witness of many individuals who have been shaped by the Lutheran Christian tradition, past and present, and in the tremendous service that has been provided to others by individuals and institutions rooted in the Lutheran understanding of faith active in love. Luther himself was humble about his role in all this. In a sermon he preached in 1522, he said, "I did nothing; the Word did everything" (LW 51:77).

May the contributions of the authors in *Together by Grace: Introducing the Lutherans* allow that same Word to work in you, its readers.

Kathryn A. Kleinhans
Waverly, Iowa
Laetare Sunday 2016

The Faith We Confess

What shaped Martin Luther's understanding of the gospel? Toward the end of his life, he reflected on a breakthrough experience he had as a young scholar. He was studying the scriptures and really wrestling with the idea of the righteousness of God. Despite his best efforts, Luther felt he could never be good enough to please God. His breakthrough came from reading Romans 1:16-17: "For I am not ashamed of the gospel; it is the power of God for salvation to everyone who has faith, to the Jew first and also to the Greek. For in it the righteousness of God is revealed through faith for faith; as it is written, 'The one who is righteous will live by faith.'" Luther suddenly realized that God's righteousness was not a standard by which God measured sinners and found them wanting but rather was a gift that God gives to us through faith in Christ. This insight revolutionized Luther's reading of the scriptures.

In a 1522 essay titled "A Brief Instruction on What to Look for and Expect in the Gospels," Luther explains his new "lens" for reading the scriptures. Don't turn Jesus into a new Moses, he writes. Instead, read the scriptures with a sense of expectation. Let the gospel be your guide. Read the scriptures in such a way that you recognize Jesus "as a gift, as a present that God has given you and that is your own" (LW 35:119). That was the good news that transformed Martin Luther, and it is the same good news that continues to transform lives today.

Luther's new insight shaped his theology. It shaped the theology of the statements of faith that guided the evolving Lutheran movement, including the Catechisms, the Augsburg Confession, and other documents that were collected and published in 1580 as *The Book of Concord*, also known as "the Lutheran Confessions." The essays in the first section of *Together by Grace* articulate this Lutheran theology as good news still for us today!

It's All about Grace

Kathryn A. Kleinhans

Each year, the students in my Lutheran heritage class at Wartburg College, Waverly, Iowa, read Martin Luther's Ninety-Five Theses. "What surprised you?" I ask them. Typically, the biggest surprise is what the Ninety-Five Theses are not: They are not a laundry list of all the things Luther didn't like about the Roman Catholic Church. What they are is an academic argument focused on one specific topic—indulgences.

Luther wasn't the first to criticize the church's use of indulgences, but he is certainly the best remembered. In 1517 he was still a fairly young professor of biblical theology at the University of Wittenberg. At the same time, a persuasive preacher named Johann Tetzel was authorized to sell indulgence letters nearby. The money received for those indulgences would finance the completion of St. Peter's Basilica in Rome, as well as expand the territory of a prominent German bishop, Albrecht of Brandenburg.

The conflict between Luther and Tetzel was the spark that ignited the Reformation. To understand the controversy, it's helpful to know some background.

The Roman Catholic Church in Luther's day distinguished between the "guilt" of sin and the "penalty" of sin. Forgiveness of guilt didn't automatically eliminate the penalty or consequence of one's sinful actions. That may sound harsh, but many parents will recognize the dynamic.

A child playing ball too close to the house breaks a window. "Of course I love you," the parent says, "and I forgive you for disobeying me. However, you'll have to do extra chores to pay for replacing the broken window." Both the forgiveness and the consequence are real. Forgiveness repairs the relationship between parent and child. But something more is required to repair the window. Until the window is actually repaired, we still live with the consequences of sin.

In the medieval sacrament of penance, Christians confessed their sins to a priest and heard the words of divine forgiveness. Their relationship with God was restored. They were also told what they were required to do as penance to make "satisfaction" for their sins. Satisfaction might involve fasting, doing good deeds, or saying a certain number of prayers. Sometimes it was easy to see the correspondence between sin and consequence.

The penalties, however, weren't always as clearly related to the sins as the example of replacing the broken window. Church leaders wrote penitential handbooks that told priests the appropriate penalties for various sins, to ensure they were fair and consistent.

Penalties and purgatory

But what if you didn't complete all your satisfaction before you died? What if you forgot to confess some of your sins and so were never even told the appropriate penance? Over time the concept of *purgatory* developed to respond to the concern that one couldn't work off the penalties of all one's sins, even during a lifetime. As long as you died forgiven, you would go to heaven, but not right away.

Only the saints—whose good works outweighed their sins—went straight to heaven. Other Christians went to purgatory first, for as long as it took to be purified or purged from the consequences of their sins. The average Christian expected this process to last thousands of years.

> **Indulgences function like extra credit—except that you can benefit from the points someone else has earned but doesn't need.**

Strange as it sounds to modern ears, purgatory was intended to be a positive, comforting idea. Let me use a classroom analogy. Penance is the makeup work a student is assigned to do to compensate for poor performance. Purgatory is like getting an "incomplete" from God at the end of the semester. It extends the time allowed for us to

The indulgences promoted by Johann Tetzel were similar to this—impressive documents, marketed in an impressive manner.

complete the work needed to pass the class.

A long, hard alternative? Yes. But the prospect of spending thousands of years in purgatory on the way to heaven was better than failure and hell.

Within this classroom analogy, indulgences function like extra credit—except that you can benefit from the points someone else has earned but doesn't need. Because the saints and Jesus had done more good than they needed for themselves, the church was able to redistribute their extra credit to others.

Basically, an indulgence was a way of transferring credit from the church's "treasury of merits" to someone else's spiritual account. Indulgences could be earned by doing certain pious deeds or by making a financial contribution to the church. They could be obtained for oneself or a loved one, even someone in purgatory.

The sale of indulgences could be overly commercialized and was often motivated by fear. Tetzel was known for his emotional slogan: "As soon as the coin in the coffer rings, the soul from purgatory springs."

But we shouldn't judge the medieval church too harshly on the basis of its excesses and abuses. In principle, the difference between receiving an indulgence because one went on a pilgrimage, for example, and receiving an indulgence letter for a monetary contribution was like the difference today between volunteering one's time to the church and writing a check to support the church's ministry. Whether one gives time, talent, or treasure is less important than the giving itself.

The gospel alternative

Luther objected to Tetzel's tactics, which he thought would lead Christians either to despair or to place their confidence in indulgences rather than in

Christ. He drafted a series of statements challenging the value of indulgences and inviting other scholars and church leaders to debate him on the topic. Although the debate never happened, Luther's Ninety-Five Theses quickly found their way to a printer and were reproduced widely.

The most powerful element of Luther's critique of indulgences is the alternative he offers. Indulgences, purgatory, penalty, and merit—the practices of the medieval church formed a complicated system. Luther cuts through all that to the gospel heart of the matter. His point is most clearly and centrally stated in thesis 62: "The true treasure of the church is the most holy gospel of the glory and grace of God."

In his explanation to the Ninety-Five Theses, Luther develops this central claim: "The gospel is a preaching of the incarnate Son of God, given to us without any merit on our part for salvation and peace. It is a word of salvation, a word of grace, a word of comfort, a word of joy."

Reflecting the widespread belief that Luther nailed his Ninety-Five Theses to the door of Wittenberg's Castle Church, the original wooden doors were replaced with these that have the Theses cast into bronze.

Luther goes on to say "that the law is fulfilled not by our works but by the grace of God . . . not through works but through faith, not by anything we offer God but by all we receive from Christ."

In other words, it's all gift! Grace isn't something that can be saved up in a treasure chest and later redistributed piece by piece. The gospel is all or nothing, a free gift with no strings attached, no hidden shipping-and-handling fees. Christ has already paid the full price. There's nothing left for us to pay or for the church to charge.

Understanding the gospel as a free gift has life-changing consequences. From the very first thesis, Luther challenges us to think—and to live—differently: "When our Lord and Master Jesus Christ said, 'Repent' [Matt. 4:17], he willed the entire life of believers to be one of repentance." This call goes deeper than ritual or emotion.

True repentance isn't about the priestly sacrament of penance (thesis 2), but it's also not simply feeling bad about one's sins (thesis 3). The Greek word for repentance, *metanoia*, describes an attitude of conversion, a fundamental reorientation of one's heart and mind. Genuine repentance is about how Christians live out our lives in the real world in response to "the true treasure" of the gospel.

> **"**
> *The gospel is all or nothing, a free gift with no strings attached, no hidden shipping-and-handling fees. Christ has already paid the full price.*
> **"**

But what does that look like? Ever the educator, Luther offers us specific examples of faithful Christian living. There's a striking pattern when you read through the entire Ninety-Five Theses. Nine of the ninety-five—that's 10 percent—begin with the words, "Christians are to be taught . . ." One of Luther's recurring themes is that Christians are to be taught to use their financial resources to care for the needs of others—both family and neighbor—rather than wasting money on indulgences.

Luther said Christian love grows when we exercise ourselves through loving actions (thesis 44). God doesn't need our good works. What God wants is our faith. It's our neighbors who need our good works.

We live lives of repentance, then, by serving others in Christ's name. The gospel takes on flesh in the day-to-day realities of our earthly lives and relationships. As Luther writes a few years later in *The Freedom of a Christian*: "A Christian lives not in himself, but in Christ and in his neighbor. He lives in Christ through faith, in his neighbor through love."

Free grace, lives of service

What can we learn from Luther's Ninety-Five Theses today? The enduring lessons are the same in 2017 as they were in 1517. The gospel of God's free grace for sinners through faith in Christ is central. Christians are to live their lives in response to this great good news, and those lives take shape in the service of neighbor.

We can also learn something from Luther's moderation. The other thing that typically surprises my students is that Luther still seems to give the pope the benefit of the doubt.

Luther criticizes the pope indirectly, saying it's hard to defend the pope's reputation from the hard questions people are asking about indulgences (theses 81–91). He insists the pope doesn't know what is being said and done in his name. If purgatory exists and if the pope could release souls from purgatory, he would do so freely, through prayer (thesis 26).

Indeed, Luther says, if the pope knew how people were being taken advantage of, he would rather see St. Peter's burn to the ground than "built up with the skin, flesh, and bones of his sheep" (thesis 50).

Is Luther sincere in these statements? Or is he being politically savvy? Perhaps he wants to offer the pope an opportunity to see himself as others do or to save face by deflecting the blame to those who claim to represent him.

Even if Luther's motives are mixed, we can learn a lesson in how to behave toward those we disagree with. Giving others the opportunity to maintain their dignity and to respond constructively is a better strategy than exposing their failings publicly.

A decade later, when Luther wrote his catechisms, we see this same attitude expressed in his explanation of the eighth commandment. As he does with each of the commandments, Luther develops a constructive behavior from the divine prohibition. The positive dimension of the commandment not to bear false witness is that the Christian should put the best construction on what our neighbor says or does.

Certainly Luther didn't always live up to that advice himself. As the Reformation continued, Luther's criticisms of his opponents became harsher and harsher. But we can still learn much from his teaching that we approach others with an attitude of generosity rather than of suspicion and blame.

Lutheranism 101: Culture or Confession?

Kathryn A. Kleinhans

What does it mean to be Lutheran? For many who have grown up Lutheran, religious identity is intertwined with a sense of family and cultural traditions: beer and brats for some, lefse and lutefisk for others, familiar liturgy and hymns for all. But the shape of Lutheranism is changing.

While the majority of Lutherans worldwide still live in northern Europe, Lutheranism is growing rapidly in other parts of the world, according to the Lutheran World Federation. Today there are almost as many Lutherans in Asia and the Middle East (7.4 million) as there are in North America (8.1 million), and there are more Lutherans in Africa (15 million) than there are in Germany (13 million).

So what does it mean to be Lutheran, beyond cultural heritage or geographical location?

During the sixteenth century, Martin Luther challenged the teachings, practices, and structures of the Roman Catholic Church. He insisted that the central message of Christianity is the good news that sinners become reconciled to God by grace through faith because of the saving work of Jesus Christ.

It's important to remember that Luther didn't intend to start a new church. He wanted to reform the existing church so that the gospel message was communicated clearly and the life of the church reflected that gospel center.

Lutherans organized into a separate church only after the Roman Catholic Church repeatedly rejected Luther's views.

"Lutheran" as insult

The word *Lutheran* actually began as an insult used by Luther's opponents. Luther later tried to discourage his supporters from calling themselves Lutherans, since they really follow Jesus Christ, not Martin Luther.

"What is Luther?" he once wrote. "After all, the teaching is not mine. Neither was I crucified for anyone."

It was the gospel message that remained central for Luther, not his leadership. In a sermon preached in Wittenberg shortly after his return from Wartburg Castle, Luther insisted: "I simply taught, preached and wrote God's word. I did nothing; the Word did everything."

If not "Lutheran," how did Luther and his supporters identify themselves and their reform movement? They tended to use the term *evangelical*, which means simply gospel or good news.

As "evangelical" Christians, they understood themselves in light of the gospel, in contrast to "papal" Christians whose identity was rooted in their relationship with church structures and authority centered in Rome, especially the pope.

One important result of this commitment to communicating the gospel clearly was that Lutherans quickly translated the scriptures and the worship service from the church's official language, Latin, into the language used by the people.

While Luther's ideas and writings were at the heart and core of this evangelical reform movement, Luther worked collaboratively with other pastors and teachers. His views also received support from civic leaders within the German territories who were interested in promoting a Christian church that was German, not Roman.

As the evangelical reform movement grew, certain writings were adopted as essential statements of Lutheranism. One of the most influential documents is the Augsburg Confession, written by Luther's colleague Philipp Melanchthon and presented at a meeting with the emperor of the Holy Roman Empire in 1530. It was signed by seven territorial rulers and by the mayors and councils of two cities.

In 1580, after both Luther's and Melanchthon's deaths, evangelical leaders gathered the statements of faith they considered normative for Lutheran Christians and published them as *The Book of Concord*. This collection was signed by fifty-one territorial rulers and by thirty-five city councils.

This act of signing one's name to a statement of faith is called *confessional subscription*. The phrase may sound odd, but the idea of a magazine or newspaper subscription is a helpful comparison. Many, many periodicals are available. We subscribe to the ones we want to receive and be engaged with regularly. To this day, Lutheran pastors and other rostered leaders promise to preach, teach, and fulfill their duties in accordance with the Lutheran confessions.

Core Lutheran themes

What are the most distinctive themes of Lutheran theology?

JUSTIFICATION BY GRACE THROUGH FAITH FOR CHRIST'S SAKE

This, for Lutherans, is the heart of the gospel. Stated concisely in the fourth article of the Augsburg Confession, it's so central that it has been called "the article by which the church stands or falls."

Both Lutherans and Roman Catholics believed God's grace was essential for salvation, but they had different understandings of the way grace works.

Relying on Paul's letters to the Romans and to the Galatians, Luther insisted that faith is key. His understanding of faith isn't primarily intellectual (having the right knowledge about God) or emotional (how hard or how sincerely one believes). Instead, faith is *relational*: It's a form of trust. We are justified through faith because faith alone trusts God's promise of forgiveness for Christ's sake.

LAW AND GOSPEL

Lutherans have a distinctive way of reading the scriptures, based on Luther's insight that God's word comes to us in two forms—law and gospel. The law as command tells people what they should do. The gospel as promise tells us what God in Christ has already done for us.

God's law functions in several ways: It structures human life by protecting and promoting good and limiting and punishing wrong. The law also functions theologically, as a mirror, or as a doctor's diagnosis, to show us our sinfulness and our need for God's grace in Christ.

Because we are sinners, God's law always accuses us; only the gospel frees us. As Luther puts it: "The law says, 'do this,' and it is never done. Grace says, 'believe in this,' and everything is already done."

MEANS OF GRACE

The Augsburg Confession describes word and sacrament as the "means of grace." Here the word "means" refers to how things actually happen. We refer to different means of communication, means of transportation, and so forth. By calling word and sacrament means of grace, we are saying: "This is how and where grace happens." When the good news is preached, when someone is baptized, when we receive the Lord's supper, grace happens.

This means that worship is vitally important for Lutherans. It forms our identity as Christians. The Augsburg Confession even defines the Christian church as the assembly of believers around gospel and sacrament.

This painting above the Theses door of the Castle Church in Wittenberg depicts the core of Lutheran theology. Christ crucified is at the center, with Martin Luther kneeling on one side holding his German translation of the Bible and Philipp Melanchthon kneeling on the other side holding the Augsburg Confession.

THEOLOGY OF THE CROSS

The theology of the cross refers not just to the events of Good Friday. It also refers to a cross-centered approach to theology that stands in opposition to a "theology of glory" focused on the power and majesty of God abstracted from God's action in history.

A theology of glory looks up and says, "God's in heaven and all's well with the world." A theology of the cross, in contrast, keeps its feet firmly planted on our broken Earth and says, "God was in Christ reconciling the world to God." The incarnation witnesses to a God who puts aside divine characteristics to become human, to suffer, and to die.

The God who chooses to come down from heaven chooses not to come down from the cross. The theology of the cross is a constant critique of human expectations. While the cross is a scandal to nonbelievers, Christians confess that God's saving power works precisely through such weakness (1 Cor. 1:23-25, 2 Cor. 12:9).

> **When the good news is preached, when someone is baptized, when we receive the Lord's supper, grace happens.**

SAINT AND SINNER

Luther described Christians as "simultaneously saint and sinner." Some religious traditions distinguish between "saints," who obey God's will, and "sinners," who disobey. Lutherans cling to a both/and understanding of Christian identity that redefines the word *saint*: a saint is a forgiven sinner.

Our dual identity as saints and sinners reminds us that our righteousness always depends on God's grace, never on our own religious behavior. At the same time, our recognition that sin, while forgiven, remains a powerful force in the world and in ourselves gives us a realistic ability to confront cruelty and evil, confident that God will have the last word.

As Luther once wrote to Melanchthon, "Be a sinner and sin boldly, but believe and rejoice in Christ even more boldly, for he is victorious over sin, death, and the world."

VOCATION

The term *vocation* literally means "calling." Until Luther's time, it was used primarily to refer to those with a special religious calling to be a priest, monk, or nun. Luther expanded the idea to include all Christians.

First, Luther affirmed that all Christians are priests. This "priesthood of all believers" doesn't mean we each have a private pipeline to God but that we all have a responsibility to teach and to pray for others.

Second, Luther affirmed that all human work is a calling from God if done in faith and for the service of neighbor. According to Luther, God doesn't need our good works, but people do. Christian faith, then, should express itself in how we live in our professions, in our family relationships, and as citizens, since these are all arenas for the service of neighbor.

Contextual theology

The Greek word *diakonos*, often translated in the New Testament as "minister" or "servant," can also refer to a waiter. This image reminds us how essential it is for the food to reach the hungry diners at the table. No matter how exquisite the chef or the food, it's no good if the meal stays in the kitchen. Similarly, the church needs to deliver the goods.

In *The Freedom of a Christian*, Luther insists that it's not enough simply to acknowledge that Christ is Christ. Instead, the purpose of preaching is to make the connection, to deliver the goods so Christ may "be Christ for you and me."

From the beginning, the Reformation was committed to delivering the goods, to continuing the work of Pentecost by allowing people to hear the good news firsthand. Luther was fluent in several languages. Even more important, he had fluency with several different populations: he wrote in Latin to reach academics and church leaders, but he wrote in German to reach regular people.

Already during Luther's lifetime, Lutheranism spread to the Scandinavian countries. Just as Luther had translated the scriptures and the worship service into German, Scandinavian evangelicals translated these—along with Luther's *Small Catechism*—into their languages.

As Lutherans came to North America, they faced several significant challenges. One was the transition away from the European model of a state-supported church. The idea of individual freedom of religion is relatively modern. After the Reformation, church and state were still integrated: The difference was that some states remained Roman Catholic while others were now Protestant.

In places where the Lutheran confession of faith was embraced, churches became national churches rather than regional branches of the Roman church.

The pluralism of the American denominational context challenged Lutherans who were used to being part of an established church. While more recent denominations like Baptists and United Methodists grew through evangelism, Lutheran church growth was largely the result of new waves of immigration from Germany and Scandinavia.

Pastor Solange Yumba Wa Nkulu of the Evangelical Lutheran Church in Congo wears a dress made from fabric designed to celebrate a church anniversary. The fabric says, in French, "Grace alone," "Scriptures alone," and "Justification by Faith, Romans 3:28."

Another challenge was the issue of cultural translation. Lutherans in the United States organized according to shared language and culture but soon found themselves asking, "What does it mean to be an American Lutheran?" What's the relationship between Lutheran confession and culture? This question shaped the self-understanding of individual communities but also affected their relationships with other Lutherans.

American Lutherans eventually overcame most of the cultural, structural, and practical issues that separated them. The Evangelical Lutheran Church in America is the result of a process of focusing increasingly on what the Augsburg Confession identifies as the core criteria for the church and its unity: the assembly of believers around word and sacrament. It's not the beer and brats or the lefse and lutefisk that unites us or divides us—it's the good news of God's grace for us in word, in water, and in bread and wine.

This focus on the core also shapes our ecumenical relationships with other Christian denominations. We aren't abandoning our identity as Lutherans. Rather, rooted in our common understanding of the gospel we are free to worship and work together with other Christians.

Unfortunately, while American Lutherans have moved beyond our ethnocentrism, we haven't been as successful in overcoming the legacy of our state-church heritage. Lutheran church membership in the United States is in a slow decline. Ironically, a church that was born "evangelical" hasn't been as intentional or effective as other denominations about actual evangelism.

> **'What does it mean to be an American Lutheran?' What's the relationship between Lutheran confession and culture?**

We can learn much from Lutherans in other cultures. What are the Lutheran churches in Tanzania and Ethiopia and elsewhere doing right? Their astonishing growth suggests they're communicating the gospel message persuasively rather than perpetuating the northern European subcultures we've too often equated with the name Lutheran.

Lutherans should welcome the opportunity to be multilingual and multicultural, to reach out actively and clearly to proclaim the good news of Jesus Christ in ways that invite other people to hear, trust, and respond to the same promise that we have received.

Lutheranism 202

Kathryn A. Kleinhans

Martin Luther (1483–1546) didn't intend to start a new church. A priest and a university professor, Luther believed there was only one Christian church. His study of the Bible and his personal faith experience led him to propose changes in the church's teaching and practice, to re-form the church so it more clearly reflected the good news of salvation through faith in Jesus Christ alone. This "reformation" was rejected by the leaders of the church in Rome, and Luther and his followers were excommunicated.

A major part of this reformation movement was an emphasis on the living, life-giving word of God. Luther's academic training was as a biblical scholar. He translated the Bible from Hebrew and Greek into German, the language of the people. He published sermons and commentaries to help communicate God's word in ways that people could understand. Most of all, Luther encouraged people to read and hear the scriptures for themselves, expecting to receive in the inspired words God's gracious promise for their lives.

Luther's ideas gained the support of many German church leaders and politicians. In 1530 these leaders presented a formal statement of their beliefs to the authorities. This statement is called the Augsburg Confession—the confession of faith made in the city of Augsburg.

In 1555, when Lutheranism finally received legal recognition within the Holy Roman Empire, it wasn't identified as "Lutheran" (followers of Martin Luther) but as "those who accept the Augsburg Confession." It was the faith, not the founder, that mattered. Still today, in countries such as Poland and

Slovakia, the Lutheran church doesn't have the word Lutheran in its name but is called the Church of the Augsburg Confession.

The Augsburg Confession highlights Luther's central insight that sinners are justified by faith:

> Furthermore, it is taught that we cannot obtain forgiveness of sin and righteousness before God by our own merit, work, or satisfactions, but that we receive forgiveness of sin and become righteous before God out of grace for Christ's sake through faith when we believe that Christ has suffered for us and that for his sake our sin is forgiven and righteousness and eternal life are given to us. [AC IV, German text]

> " *'Out of grace for Christ's sake through faith' . . . has been called 'the article by which the church stands or falls.'* "

The point is not just that we have faith, since one can have faith in anything—a friend or family member, one's own ability, a sports team. Christians aren't justified by the strength or sincerity of our belief but by the one in whom we believe. Only faith in Christ restores our relationship with God, because such faith trusts the promises God has made—and kept—in the death and resurrection of Jesus.

"Out of grace for Christ's sake through faith"—this is so central to the way Lutherans think about the Christian faith that it has been called "the article by which the church stands or falls."

Such faith

But justification by faith alone is not the last word that Luther and the Confessions have for us. It's only the beginning of the Lutheran understanding of Christian life. Faith in Christ isn't just about what happens when we die. It's about how we live. And it's about how we live not just for ourselves but for and with others.

One way of thinking about what Lutherans believe is to visualize justification by faith alone as the center of a flower, from which all the petals unfold, or as the hub of a wheel, from which the spokes radiate out. Without the center, without the hub, all you have is a bunch of disconnected parts. With the right center, everything else falls into place. Everything else in the Augsburg Confession—sin, the sacraments, worship, married clergy, the role of bishops—everything else is developed in relation to the core belief of justification by faith alone.

When we look at other parts of the Augsburg Confession, we see clearly how this interrelationship unfolds. Immediately following Article IV on justifying faith, Article V (the office of the ministry) tells us where "such faith" comes from, and Article VI (the new obedience) tells us what "such faith" does.

> To obtain such faith God instituted the office of preaching, giving the gospel and the sacraments. Through these, as through means, he gives the Holy Spirit who produces faith, when and where he wills, in those who hear the gospel. [AC V, German text]

This assertion challenges the view that faith is simply my own private connection to God. Have you ever heard someone say, "I can worship God just fine on a golf course on Sunday morning"? It's true that I can praise God's marvelous works as Creator when I sit on a mountaintop or watch a sunset or even play golf. But those experiences tell only part of the story. They don't communicate the great good news that God in Christ is Savior—my Savior—as well as Creator.

"How Great Thou Art" is true, but it's incomplete unless I can also sing "Jesus loves me!" Lutherans call word and sacrament "the means of grace" because they point to where and how God ministers to us with the promise of forgiveness through Jesus Christ. Worship serves as our response to God only after God's gracious initiative first reaches out to us.

Luther knew firsthand how easy it is to get trapped in our own mental and spiritual ruts. He insisted that the word of God comes to us from outside ourselves, breaking into our sinful self-centeredness. We hear God's gracious "for you" most clearly when we hear it in a voice other than our own. We feel God's gracious "for you" when we are splashed with water from the font. When we taste the bread and wine, we confess that Christ is really present, his own body and blood giving life to ours.

We all know the difference between things that operate on battery power and those that must be plugged in. When the battery runs down, you recharge it or get a new one. But while the battery is working, you're good to go on your own.

Christian faith isn't battery operated. We don't just recharge every week and then go out on our own. Faith plugs us in to an ongoing relationship with Jesus Christ. We have power because his power flows through us.

To use a more organic image, Jesus told his followers to abide in him, as branches are rooted in a vine. Cut them off from the vine, and they wither and die. "Apart from me you can do nothing," Jesus says, in one of the most frequently quoted passages in the Lutheran Confessions (John 15:5).

Personal, never private

Hearing God's word preached and sharing in God's sacraments—these aren't things we can do on our own, on the golf course or on a mountaintop. Faith requires the gathering of the Christian community, the ministry—God's ministry to us—of word and sacrament. Christian faith is deeply personal but never private.

Sometimes the Lutheran emphasis on faith alone has led us to avoid talking about works, as if what we actually do as Christians isn't important. It's easy to contrast faith and works, as if they were opposites. But that was never Luther's point. What he criticized was *not* doing good but rather relying on one's actions to improve one's status with God.

According to Augsburg Confession, Article VI:

> It is also taught that such faith should yield good fruit and good works and that a person must do such good works as God has commanded for God's sake but not place trust in them as if thereby to earn grace before God. [AC VI, German text]

Baptism at Bethany Lutheran Church, Crystal Lake, Illinois.

Faith alone—only faith—justifies. But in the Christian life, faith never is alone. In his lectures on Genesis, Luther wrote, "We know indeed that faith is never alone but brings with it love and other manifold gifts." In his preface to the New Testament, Luther described faith as "a living, busy, active, mighty thing." He said, "It is impossible to separate works from faith, quite as impossible as to separate heat and light from fire."

This is what's "new" about the new obedience. The works done by Christians are an inevitable outgrowth of their faith in Christ. As Jesus said, a good tree bears good fruit. Christians don't do good works because they are instructed to do so; Christians do good works when they are filled with a living faith in Christ. When we trust God's gracious promise, serving others is no longer a "got to" but a "get to."

> "
> *Faith alone—only faith—justifies. But in the Christian life, faith never is alone.*
> "

And if faith is never alone, so, too, the believer is never alone. God's grace turns us outward toward others. Luther describes the relationship between faith and works in the context of our relationships with God and neighbor. God deals with us, Luther says, "through a word of promise." We deal with God "through faith in the word of his promise." And we deal with others "on the basis of works." God comes to us, in word and sacrament, in Jesus himself. And through us God reaches out to others.

Faith at work

Lutherans have a long, strong history of combining evangelistic outreach and social ministry activity, working both to spread the faith and to make faith active in loving service of others. Wherever they are, wherever they go, Lutherans build schools and establish networks of care.

August Hermann Francke, a pastor and professor at the University of Halle in Germany from 1691 to 1727, was an early leader in Lutheran social ministry. Francke founded an orphanage, a school for the poor, a school for girls, a teacher-training institute, a medical dispensary, and more. King Frederick William I of Prussia was so impressed by his visit to Halle that he used Francke's ideas as a model for reform throughout his realm.

Francke also made Halle a center of foreign missions. The first Lutheran missionary ever, Bartholomäus Ziegenbalg, was sent to South India from Halle in 1706. Henry Melchior Muhlenberg came to Pennsylvania from Halle in 1742 to help organize and strengthen American Lutherans.

In the middle of the nineteenth century, Wilhelm Loehe, a pastor in the remote Bavarian village of Neuendettelsau, established a deaconess training program, hospitals, and schools to meet the needs of his region, as well as a mission society that sent pastors to North and South America, Australia, and New Guinea.

We have similar examples today. I live in Waverly, Iowa, a town of nine thousand people. Waverly is home not only to two ELCA congregations and the Northeastern Iowa Synod office but also to a Lutheran school (kindergarten through sixth grade), Wartburg College, Lutheran Services in Iowa, and Bartels Lutheran Retirement Community. In previous generations an orphanage and a Lutheran insurance company were located here. When Lutherans came to Waverly they didn't just build a church. Over the years they built a community infrastructure that still remains.

When record-breaking floods ravaged the Midwest in the summer of 2008, Lutheran Disaster Response was here, working in cooperation with

Lutheran Services in Iowa—just as it had been in the aftermath of spring tornadoes. Wartburg College stepped forward to offer space as a Red Cross shelter and to coordinate volunteer cleanup efforts. Why? Because Lutherans practice what we preach—putting faith into action in servant love of neighbor. "Such faith" in Christ prompts us to reach out to our neighbors, known and unknown.

Through the prophet Isaiah, God promises: "When you pass through the waters, I will be with you; and through the rivers, they shall not overwhelm you; when you walk through fire you shall not be burned, and the flame shall not consume you" (Isa. 43:2). When literal waters did overwhelm many of us, living waters reminded us of our baptism. When wildfires threatened others, the flames of the Spirit strengthened us. For we believe that nothing can finally overcome those who are joined together in the body of Christ. Such faith, nurtured through word and sacrament, bears fruit in God's word.

As the ELCA so powerfully puts it: "God's work. Our hands." Thanks be to God!

Read the Bible with Martin Luther

R. Guy Erwin

D o you want to sing, shout, and leap for joy in the gospel of Jesus Christ? That's how Martin Luther told readers of his revised edition of the Bible in 1545 they ought to feel when they sat down to read it: "It is good news, a great shout resounding through all the world," shared by prophets and apostles and all who seek within its pages the consolation, strength, and victory offered in it by God.

Luther was, in many ways, his own best example of this joy in the biblical text. His passion to communicate its saving message infused and enlivened the whole of his commentary, his preaching, and his theological writing.

Luther's entire stormy public career, in fact, can be directly connected to his deep study, analysis, proclamation, and translation of the biblical text. Modern Lutherans share this legacy. Our tradition of Bible study and reading—from the humblest kitchen table to the most scholarly library—has been powerfully shaped by Luther's conviction that it is in the text of the Bible that God's saving message to humankind has been most faithfully, effectively, and enduringly communicated.

But Luther has more to teach us than simply to treasure the Bible and to read it. He has also given us a way of reading and listening to scripture that is distinctive and powerful and, at the same time, helps steer us away from arrogance and presumption and self-righteousness.

Luther's most intensive early exposure to the biblical text came after he was accepted as a novice by the Augustinian monastery in Erfurt, Germany. In a strict monastery life, the whole Psalter would be prayed in the course of every week. In penitential seasons Bible reading was a regular part of an Augustinian friar's personal devotion. We know that as a novice Luther enjoyed the rare luxury (for his time) of having a Bible just for his own use.

Luther's gift for study and analysis so impressed his superiors that he was chosen for graduate study at Wittenberg, intended to lead to a job as a professor of biblical studies. It's in these early years of intensive study and the beginning of his teaching career that the Bible became Luther's central focus—and it's when he began to develop the insights that would later make him controversial.

"Luther Discovers the Bible," by nineteenth-century painter Ferdinand Pauwels, portrays Martin Luther studying the Bible as a young monk.

Radical reassessment

Particularly in his early lectures on the Psalms and Romans, Luther gradually came to understand the scriptural message in a way that differed from the prevailing tradition. This would lead him both to a radical reassessment of the Bible's basic message and to a strong critique of his contemporaries' way of reading and interpreting it.

In his study and teaching of Paul's letters, Luther came to understand the path to salvation as something very different from what had been commonly taught in the church. It was not something to be earned through piety, use of the sacraments, good behavior, and avoidance of sin. It was a gift of God offered freely in Christ and testified to by Paul's teaching that the saved are judged righteous by God through grace manifested in faith. This God-given grace was not the result of an accumulation of good works but was entirely apart from any human deserving or merit.

> **"**
> **In his study and teaching of Paul's letters, Luther came to understand the path to salvation as something very different from what had been commonly taught in the church.**
> **"**

As a result of this insight, the whole of scripture seemed to Luther suddenly to communicate a different message than he had previously learned and taught. No longer just a book of laws and judgment, the Bible's whole message became for Luther a word of grace and redemption. His insight was to change forever the way he and his followers—and the millions of Christian heirs of the Reformation today—read the Bible.

Word and words

In his maturity as a theologian, Luther came to see the whole of scripture through a pair of interpretive lenses: first, the idea of the Word of God as Jesus—the Word made flesh—as distinct from the words of the biblical text; then, in the special relationship between law and gospel, as ways of communicating the divine message of grace.

The first of these led Luther to distinguish sharply between the content of the message and its medium. For Luther the text of scripture is holy not because of its origin but because of the message of divine favor it contains. Even the claim of the Hebrew Bible to speak for God would, for example, not make it the "Bible" for Christians if it didn't also in some way witness to

Christ. In believing that it did, Luther was part of a long tradition of Christian reinterpretation of the Hebrew scriptures.

But it's the New Testament that, for Luther, sets the whole understanding of God's revelation to God's people—first in a person, then in a text—as a story of the incarnation, life, death, and resurrection of Jesus, and as a proclamation of salvation offered freely to humans redeemed by grace. Luther was fond of saying that the text of the Bible was like the swaddling clothes or the manger in which the baby Jesus was laid—not God itself but the trusty bearer of God for us—enclosing, protecting, and cradling the true Word.

Jesus, the incarnate Word, is for Luther always the center, subject, and meaning of the scripture's many words: the inner Word of God preserved and communicated in the outer, visible words of scripture. This gives Luther a distinctive interpretive angle: What shows us Jesus in the scriptures communicates God's favor; and what does not shows us only human weakness and limitation.

Luther's other great contribution to our way of reading the Bible came through his identification of the tension between law and gospel he finds running through it. Again, this isn't just a simple distinction between the Old and New Testaments but a subtle and profound recognition of the way God communicates with God's people in scripture both through texts that frighten and judge and those that reassure and relieve.

Seeing the Bible's message as both a message of judgment and a message of forgiveness at the same time made it possible for Luther to reconcile apparently impossible differences between the Hebrew scriptures and the New Testament writings.

"Gospel" in ten commandments

Suddenly, for Luther, the "law" and the "gospel" both appear—simultaneously, side by side or parallel—everywhere in scripture, both in the writings of the ancient law and in Jesus' teaching of acceptance and peace.

All at once the ten commandments become for Luther gospel as much as they are obviously law: law in the sense that they demonstrate to an erring humankind the impossibility of achieving even the most basic of God's commands; gospel in that they show God's love for humankind, a love that sees human achievement not in the sense of "earning salvation" but as serving our neighbor.

In the first commandment, for example, "I am the Lord your God" is *at the same time* a terrifying judgment (I, not you, am God; I am above you and judge of your failings) and thus law; *and* the ultimate consolation and relief (I, not you, am God; you belong to me completely and I love you) and thus gospel.

This simultaneity of judgment and redemption is for Luther a basic way the Bible communicates God's Word, and this insight makes it possible for him to read even the scriptures of ancient Judaism as part of the gospel message made flesh in Jesus Christ.

Not every part of the biblical text is capable of being read in this way, of course, but this law/gospel interpretive scheme helped Luther—and helps us—distinguish the Bible's central texts and messages from ones that are more peripheral and less important.

> "
> *Luther was fond of saying that the text of the Bible was like the swaddling clothes or the manger in which the baby Jesus was laid—not God itself but the trusty bearer of God for us—enclosing, protecting, and cradling the true Word.*
> "

Luther used his insights boldly. He was a fearless judge of scripture. With an astounding assurance, he elevated some parts of the Bible to great importance, while relegating others to relative insignificance.

Confident in the usefulness of all ancient texts in some way or another, Luther resisted the temptation to remove the later texts of the Jewish tradition we now call the Apocrypha (which had been part of Christian Bibles from earliest times) from his Bible translations. But he separated them from the other Old Testament texts and introduced them as not equal in value with the other books of the old covenant.

Many later Protestants removed the Apocrypha altogether, but Luther continued to see value in it. The official translations of the Bible used by Lutheran churches in Europe often still contain it.

More daring yet, Luther described some New Testament books as clearly more valuable than the others, particularly the Gospel of John, Paul's letters to the Romans, Galatians, and Corinthians, and Peter's letters. He was famously dismissive of others, particularly the Letter of James, because of the weakness of their message about Christ.

Revelation: Don't read it alone

He even suggested that Revelation not be read by individual Christians because of the possibility they might become distracted by its drama, take it too literally, and begin to wonder when the events it describes would come to pass.

Luther was empowered to such freedom in scriptural interpretation not only because of his theological insights about justification, Jesus as the incarnation of the Word, and the distinction between law and gospel, but also because of his experience as a translator of the biblical text.

The very act of choosing German words to represent religious ideas he knew only from Latin, Greek, and Hebrew texts was daring. Luther's skill and insight led him to create a translation that still has power and grandeur today, and which was instrumental in the formation of the modern German language.

But, as Luther came to know well, translating is always a matter of judgment. And the way he recast the ancient texts into a new language tended to reinforce the theological understanding of the biblical text he had already developed. In some instances, Luther's translation was criticized both by Roman Catholics and by more radical Protestants as being theologically self-serving.

Luther never saw the task of biblical translation as one that could be completely finished. Throughout his lifetime he continued to revise and improve on his translation, with the help of his Wittenberg colleagues and friends.

Lutheran "spin" in translation?

Luther also wrote introductions to many of the Bible's books, in which he gave their contents a particular Lutheran "spin" and provided marginal notes explaining particularly "dark" (his word) passages or terms.

In his 1545 instructions, Luther makes it clear that the main purpose of such devotional reading is to unlock the personal promise of grace—to discover, in the general revelation of God's favor toward humankind shown in Jesus, the personal aspect, the "for me"—through which the Spirit illumines the reader's heart and makes her a believer.

This illumination in the Spirit, through which our understanding that what Jesus does by living and dying for the world becomes a personal truth, is thus God's work, not our own.

The announcement of this truth and its application to the individual believer are—in Luther's view—the whole purpose of the Bible, the church's proclamation, its preaching, and its sacraments. He insists that this personal appropriation of God's promise shown in Christ is the ultimate "good news," what he calls the "great shout" of the gospel.

But reading the Bible, like any human activity, is subject to temptation and weakness. And in Luther's view, the main human temptation in Bible reading is the same as in daily life: self-centeredness leading to self-righteousness. Reading the Bible to reinforce one's sense of "rightness" by looking for laws to follow and by which to judge others is, in Luther's view, vain and wrong.

Although Christians should know better, Luther insists, it remains a grave temptation even to believers to make laws out of God's promises and to forget that the gospel message is one of forgiveness, acceptance, and grace.

Although the giving of law was once an important aspect of the Old Testament, for Luther the purpose of those laws is now

> "
> *Readers of the Bible, sing, leap, and shout for joy!*
> "

to make clear the human need for God's grace, represented by Jesus, the Word made flesh. His particular concern is that readers not make laws out of Jesus' message and teachings in the New Testament, since Jesus came not to establish law but to fulfill it and to liberate believers from the law's burden.

In fact, Luther was quite prescriptive about what he believed private reading of the Bible was for and clear as to how it should be done.

His instructions to readers grew naturally out of his theological development, his reforming agenda, and the negative experience he was having with critics of his thought from the Roman and the radical reforming directions. Both of these (though in very different ways) tended to see the Bible first as a source of laws and ordinances and then only secondarily, if at all, as a liberating and empowering text.

That won't sound unfamiliar even today, when the human impulse to seek comfort in the clarity of law is still strong and the gospel's promise of freedom is often avoided as an invitation to a path unknown. But as Luther taught—and Lutherans still believe—there is no surer and more trustworthy promise than the freedom from sin, death, and the devil that God offers in the gospel to which the scriptures testify.

So, readers of the Bible, sing, leap, and shout for joy!

For further reading

Timothy J. Wengert. *Reading the Bible with Martin Luther: An Introductory Guide.* Grand Rapids, MI: Baker Academic, 2013.

Discipleship and Spirituality According to Luther's Catechisms

Edward H. Schroeder

In 1529 Martin Luther wrote two catechisms. He did so after a survey was made in congregations in Saxony in 1528. In this "Saxon Visitation" seminary professors from Wittenberg (Luther too) went out into the towns and villages to listen and learn what was actually happening in the preaching and teaching in the congregations. What they discovered was bad news. Many people in the congregations, and many pastors too, did not know basic Christianity. In the preface to the Small Catechism, Luther wrote: "Good God, what wretchedness I beheld! The common people . . . have no knowledge whatever of Christian teaching, and unfortunately many pastors are quite incompetent." With his two catechisms—small for laity, large for clergy—Luther offers help to improve the sad situation.

There was a long tradition of catechisms in the Western, Latin-speaking church. They usually had three parts: Apostles' Creed, Lord's Prayer, Ten Commandments, usually in that order. Luther changed the order in his catechisms, but, more important, he changed the theology underlying all parts of the catechism. He also added three more parts: Baptism, the Lord's Supper, and Private Confession and Absolution. Luther's original discovery, his "breakthrough," as he called it, for reading the Bible, was that God speaks two different "words" in the Bible: God's word of law and God's word of gospel (often called "God's word of promise"). Law and gospel are

Reproduction of the title page of Luther's Small Catechism (1529).

two words from the same God to the same human beings, but as different as death and life, night and day. Law is God's requirement. Its primary verb is "require." God's law requires that we do (or don't do) this or that. The gospel is God's gift. Its primary verb is "offer." God offers—as a gift—his mercy and forgiveness. Luther's catechisms apply this distinction between law and gospel in all six parts.

Previous catechisms used in the Western church did not know that distinction. They taught the creed, the Lord's Prayer, and the commandments as revelations of God's will for Christians: what people *ought* to believe, how they *ought* to pray, and how they *should* behave. Those three texts touched the basic areas of a Christian's life—faith, worship, and ethics; or the mind, the heart, and the hand; or thinking, feeling, and acting. But the language of "should" and "ought" made the entire catechism to be God's law—things God required people to do. That is not good news for sinners, not gospel.

Luther begins both catechisms with the ten commandments, not the creed. But he does not present the ten commandments as ethics. Instead the commandments are God's word for diagnosis, God's X-ray, to show us our sin, our sickness. They do tell us what we should do, but they show us that we are not doing what we should be doing. They show us that our person (inside), not just our action (outside), needs to be changed. They show us the path we should take in life, but they do so to show us that we are already off the path and going in some other direction.

One commandment to guide them all

The first commandment, said Luther, is really the only commandment there is. "The First Commandment is the chief source and fountainhead that permeates all others; again, to it they all return and upon it they depend, so that the end and beginning are completely linked and bound together."[1] The other nine commandments actually "repeat" this first one—we should fear, love, and trust in God—in these other areas of our life. But even with all their godliness, the ten commandments are not good news for sinners. None of us (on the inside) is fearing, loving, and trusting God in all areas of our life "with all our heart, all our mind, all our strength" all the time. We're all first-commandment-breakers.

In Luther's catechisms, good news does not come until we get to the Apostles' Creed. And even there the heart of the gospel's good news is not present in the creed's first article. The first article says God is our creator and that everything we have is a gift from God. That sure sounds good. But these gifts put us under obligations ("oughts") that we can never fulfill. That fact is often "softened" in some translations of Luther's words here. For example, what I memorized in my childhood was: "For all of this [all the gifts of creation that God has given me] it is my duty to thank and to praise, to serve and obey God. This is most certainly true." That suggests that the "duty" is doable. What Luther's German actually says is much more drastic: "For all this I am already in arrears, way behind in my obligations, to thank and to praise, to serve and obey God. This is most certainly true!" Even the first article of the Apostles' Creed concerning creation leaves us guilty before God.

Finding the good news

Only when we come to the second article of the creed ["I believe in Jesus Christ"] does the good news begin. In this article the confession is simple: Jesus Christ is my Lord. Lord means owner, Luther says. "My Lord" means the one to whom I belong. The biographical elements in the second article of the creed are the means by which he became "my" Lord and made me his "own."

After the second article of the creed all the remaining parts of the catechism are good news—the creed's third article, then the Lord's Prayer, and then the three items Luther added in his catechism: Baptism, the Lord's Supper, and Confession and Absolution.

---

1. Robert Kolb and Timothy J. Wengert, *The Book of Concord: The Confessions of the Evangelical Lutheran Church* (Minneapolis: Fortress Press, 2000), 430.

The creed's third article is the "good news" about God's work (through the Holy Spirit and the church) to connect people today to Jesus Christ as Lord. It tells how sinners today receive the good news they need to survive in the face of God's X-ray report about them.

The Lord's Prayer is good news for practicing our trust in Christ and for receiving God's continual care and blessings in the struggle of daily life, a struggle articulated in the seven different areas of the seven petitions of the Lord's Prayer.

Baptism, Lord's supper, and confession and absolution are three resources (means of grace) that God supplies for keeping us connected to Christ in our struggle to live by faith in daily life. In these additional parts to the catechisms Luther's emphasis is not so much on correct teaching about these three means of grace, but the best way to use all three for daily life. Here is Luther's gift for discipleship and spirituality.

"Using" baptism means dying and rising with Christ every day that we live, facing temptation and tough situations with the words: "I am baptized!"

"Using" the Lord's supper means receiving it often and hearing the words "given and shed for you." You are "worthy" (prepared) for it simply by admitting that you need Christ, and trusting his promise coming to you in the Lord's supper.

"Using" confession and absolution means actually doing it, so that the burden of our daily sinning is taken away and we hear Christ's word of forgiveness with our own name included: "Ed, by Christ's command I announce to you the forgiveness of the sin(s) you have just confessed." It's like dying and rising again, like baptism.

Living Luther's theology

Now let's connect Luther's catechism theology to discipleship and spirituality.

Christian discipleship, being a disciple of Jesus Christ, means saying yes to Jesus' invitation, "Follow me." In the catechism Luther makes one point central: "Jesus Christ is *my* Lord." In the New Testament that same confession is at the center of discipleship. What kind of lordship is that? One important text is Matthew 20:24-28, where Jesus specifies that his authority is not authority over, but authority under, supporting, sustaining his disciples all the way to giving his life as a ransom "for many." What kind of "following" comes from that sort of lordship? Theologian Dietrich Bonhoeffer articulated it this way: "When our Lord Christ bids us come and follow him, he bids us come and die with him." We all do die. But there are two ways to do it. One is clutching what we have "for dear life" and dying that way. The other is clinging to Christ (and his gospel) and dying that way. Disciples of Christ, said Luther, are "little Christs."

Christian spirituality in New Testament language is "being led by the Holy Spirit." Not all references in the scriptures to God's Spirit are speaking of the "Holy" Spirit. "Spirit," both in Hebrew and in Greek, is the word for wind, for breath. It signals power—to move things, to make alive. Even apart from Christ, God's power operates in the cosmos—as Luther's explanation to the first article of the creed shows. When the New Testament speaks of the "Holy" Spirit, the adjective adds something very specific. My late colleague Bob Bertram put it this way: the Holying Spirit is the Healing Spirit, the spirit sinners need to survive, to be re-enlivened with God's own Wind—and not simply "blown away." Therefore, no surprise, when New Testament writers speak of that Holying Spirit, it is always connected to Christ. "Life in the Spirit" comes when Christians are "led by the Holy Spirit," and that Spirit's leading

> **The focus of Luther's catechisms is living by faith in Christ out in the world of daily work and daily callings.**

always leads us to Christ. So the explanation of the creed's third article in the Small Catechism goes like this: "I believe that by my own understanding or strength I cannot believe in Jesus Christ my Lord, or come to him, but instead the Holy Spirit . . . calls, gathers, enlightens, and makes holy the whole Christian church on earth and keeps it with Jesus Christ in the one, common, true faith."[2] Christian spirituality is living 24/7 "in union with Jesus Christ."

Especially in the Gospel of John, this Christ-connecting agenda of the Holy Spirit is driven home over and over again. The Holy Spirit "will not speak on his own, but will take what is mine and declare it to you." And Paul is not far behind, for example, in Galatians 5 where "belonging to Christ Jesus" and "living by the Spirit" and "being led by the Spirit" are all synonyms.

---

2. *Book of Concord*, 355–56.

For both discipleship and spirituality, the focus of Luther's catechisms is living by faith in Christ out in the world of daily work and daily callings. It is a clear alternative, even antithesis, to the monastic heritage of Luther's early adult years: not withdrawing from daily life's realities for spiritual agendas, but taking Christ-connected faith out into the worldly agendas where God has placed me. Jesus' final words to Peter in John's gospel (21:18-19) push the point: even as you are taken "where you do not wish to go," even there, "Follow me." There is no worldly turf that is off limits for "following Christ as Lord" and being "led by the Spirit."

From the Sixteenth Century to Today

The Reformation was not the work of a single individual, not even one as gifted as Martin Luther. Luther had many collaborators in the work of reform. Other scholars developed Luther's understanding of the gospel. Other church leaders implemented Luther's ideas in congregations. Luther's wife created a home—and guest house—that supported his work, both emotionally and financially. Subsequent generations carried on the work of the sixteenth-century reformers, spreading the Lutheran understanding of Christianity throughout the world.

Several of the essays in this section of *Together by Grace* introduce you to people who played essential roles in the beginnings of the Reformation: Martin Luther himself, his wife, Katharina von Bora Luther, and his colleagues Philipp Melanchthon and Johannes Bugenhagen. Other essays explore the spread of the Lutheran movement, both globally and to the United States in particular. The final essays in this section introduce you to two Lutherans who achieved prominence on a world stage: twentieth-century theologian Dietrich Bonhoeffer and twenty-first century peace activist Leymah Gbowee, whose faith motivated them to act for the benefit of others in situations of horrifying violence and oppression. Both are witnesses to the continuing legacy of the Reformation and to the power of God's word unleashed in the world.

Martin Luther (1483–1546)

Robert Kolb

Five hundred years have passed since the Wittenberg professor and Augustinian friar Martin Luther began to make headlines, and he is still at it! In November 1517, his Ninety-Five Theses on indulgences (a remission of temporal punishment in purgatory for sins committed during one's life) appeared in print, pirated by printers taking a risk by presenting an academic invitation to discussion for a wider public. The sale of the theses revealed a previously unrecognized market for a few imaginative printers. Luther himself went on to develop the potential of Johann Gutenberg's invention of movable type through effective use of several literary genres. Luther also expanded and heightened the role of oral proclamation, which had been subordinated to sacred ritual in medieval religious practice. Both his instruction in Wittenberg lecture halls and others reading his writings

A Timeline of Martin Luther's Life

1483	**Born in Eisleben**
1505	**Enters monastery in Erfurt**
1508	**Arrives in Wittenberg**
1512	**Receives doctoral degree**
1517	**Posts Ninety-Five Theses**
1521	**Excommunicated and outlawed**
1521–22	**At the Wartburg Castle**
1522	**Publishes German translation of New Testament**
1525	**Marries Katharina von Bora**
1534	**Publishes German translation of the Bible**
1546	**Dies in Eisleben**

across and beyond German lands sparked profound changes in the way Christians understood their religion.

Parents, priests, and professors had all impressed on Luther that key to the practice of the Christian faith was the human performance of good deeds—above all, religious works or sacred activities—even if God's help was needed to initiate or perfect those works. Luther's volatile personality allowed him to be brutally honest about his own failings, depriving him of all inner peace and hope. Instructors from the schools of thought initiated by William of Ockham (ca. 1297–1347) shaped Luther's theology negatively by emphasizing the necessity of human

> **"**
> *Professor Luther's understanding of being Christian was transformed as he began his teaching career with lectures on the Psalms and then Romans, Galatians, and Hebrews.*
> **"**

merit for salvation, alongside God's grace, but implanted in him an image of God as almighty Creator. Professor Luther's understanding of being Christian was transformed as he began his teaching career with lectures on the Psalms and then Romans, Galatians, and Hebrews. There he found that God initiates and sustains the relationship between God and God's people through speaking. God's word, in oral, written, and sacramental forms, sustains and completes that relationship. God's children rest in their Creator's hand. Against his despair now fought a powerful joy over God's ardent and unstoppable love, demonstrated in Christ's death and resurrection for *him*, Martin Luther.

God's good news for sinners

After he had formulated his foundation for interpreting scripture, Luther began to develop that message for a wider public when he was called before his fellow Augustinian brothers at Heidelberg in April 1518. He did not discuss indulgences or the question of papal authority that his Ninety-Five Theses had raised but instead presented his "theology of the cross." Papal authority was placed on his agenda in 1519, however, in the Leipzig Debate by the leading defender of medieval theology in Germany, Johann Eck. For the rest of his life, Luther wanted to talk about God's speaking to sinners and re-creating them as beloved children through the liberating death and

In Worms, Germany, Luther appeared before the imperial assembly, or "diet," and at least in deed said, "Here I stand." Four contemporary Christians take their stand at the same spot.

resurrection of Christ and through the Holy Spirit's delivering all the good things Christ's work makes possible through God's word—above all, forgiveness of sins, life, and salvation, the life restored to God's original plan. But Luther's opponents forced him also to examine in detail the abuses of medieval church leadership and teaching so that he could redirect the faith of God's people to Jesus.

After the Leipzig Debate, the papal judicial machinery ground out threats and then condemnation of Luther's ideas and finally, in early 1521, personal excommunication. After Luther had confessed his faith before the imperial legislative assembly (called a "diet") in Worms, Charles V, the German emperor, declared him an outlaw. Luther's ruler, Elector Frederick the Wise of Saxony, kidnapped him to protect him from execution by church or imperial government. While hiding in the Wartburg Castle, Luther translated the New Testament with the aid of the first printed edition of the Greek New Testament, produced five years earlier by the learned biblical scholar Desiderius Erasmus, of Rotterdam. Luther's translation launched a rise in biblical literacy to heights previously unknown. From the Wartburg, Luther also launched the first continuing education program for priests, beginning what became a series of "postils," collections of sermons on the appointed lessons for the Sundays and festivals of the church year, to aid priests in learning how to preach the gospel and thus to serve as the Holy Spirit's instruments in cultivating trust in Christ. Even though he thought God's word addresses individuals best in oral and sacramental forms of the promise, Luther strengthened the ability of individual believers, families, and pastors to deliver the message of Christ through his written works.

Luther expands on his vision

Between June 1520 and January 1522 Luther had produced a series of major works on fundamental topics involved in his proposals for reform of church and society: *On Good Works, The Open Letter to the German Nobility, On the Babylonian Captivity of the Church, The Freedom of the Christian*, the *Confutation of Latomus*, and *On Monastic Vows*. His return to Wittenberg in 1522 and to the classroom two years later began twenty years of teaching, preaching, writing, and counseling that embedded his vision of Christian trust in Christ and the joyful new obedience that trust produces in the minds and hearts of theological colleagues and simple children.

Distractions of various kinds and supportive teamwork from colleagues and friends across German lands and beyond marked those two decades.

> **Katharina von Bora ... became manager of his household, curate of his troubled soul, companion during often troubled times, and mother of their six children.**

Several turning points occurred in 1525. Peasant revolts had threatened to bring chaos to society over the past quarter century, so when in late 1524 widespread armed strife broke out in many German lands, pitting peasant groups against secular authorities, Luther was drawn into public discussion. He justified the peasant protests against injustice, for he was sharply critical throughout his life of abuses of power by leaders of governments. But he feared the terror and tyranny of the mob as well and saw no orderly governing of society emerging from peasant revolts. Although it is often said that his stance against the revolts cost him popular support, his reform movement continued to spread, also among the common people, with little interruption. A more positive turning point came in June 1525 when he married Katharina von Bora, who had escaped the cloistered life and successfully wooed him. She became manager of his household, curate of his troubled soul, companion during often troubled times, and mother of their six children. The children provided delight and lessons in life for their parents. Particularly the deaths of two daughters, Elizabeth and Magdalena, afflicted the reformer with deep grief, of which he wrote movingly.

The death of his protector, Elector Frederick the Wise, provided a turning point as well. Frederick's brother and successor, John ("the Steadfast"), abandoned Frederick's public silence on Luther's message. He actively supported the Wittenberg Reformation, initiated a visitation of congregations that aided the introduction of reform locally, and enjoyed a warm personal relationship with Luther, his family, and his colleagues.

Hanging over him during 1525 was Erasmus's attack on Luther's understanding that sin binds human choice and prevents any human contribution at all to deliverance from alienation from God. Erasmus's relationship with his younger Wittenberg contemporary had always had two edges. Erasmus's view of necessary reform concentrated on institutional and moral change. He did not understand Luther's doctrinal concerns, nor did he share Luther's passion for assuring troubled consciences that their relationship with God was totally God's gift. Luther believed that the Holy Spirit creates the faith that clings to Christ, and Christ alone guarantees the promise of life with God forever. This conflict resulted, after a year's hesitation, in Luther's composing *On Bound Choice* (often translated *On the Bondage of the Will*), a work that has received much attention and no little misinterpretation in the last century, but that made only small ripples in its time. Its chief impact was that it drew many of Erasmus's young followers into Luther's train.

Companions in teaching and life

In all this, Luther did not stand alone. In addition to his wife, Katharina, at his side, his movement prospered because of the team that assembled around him, colleagues and students in Wittenberg, and others in parishes across German-speaking territories, who wrote and preached and negotiated and instituted new forms for worship and life in the church. Most important of these were his colleagues, foremost, Philipp Melanchthon, a genius in many ways, along with Johannes Bugenhagen, Justus Jonas, and Caspar Cruciger. He also interacted with artists such as Lucas Cranach, a dozen or more printers in Wittenberg and others beyond, courtiers, leading citizens, and many others. Particularly his students were important as aids in developing his ideas through conversation around his table in the evenings and in some cases as faithful editors of his works.

Biblical lectures, hundreds of letters of counsel and consolation, devotional works, and other treatises mark Luther's last two decades. Most important in these years was his authorship of his catechism—the medieval word for basic instruction in the Christian faith, which had taken place largely in sermons. Luther took advantage of the advance of the culture of print and placed that instruction into two forms. His Large Catechism contained sermons on the core curriculum, the ten commandments, the creed, and the Lord's Prayer, with sermons on the sacraments as well. His Small Catechism placed that curriculum into the minds of children, in memorable questions and answers, and then demonstrated how to live out the life that his summary of the biblical message impels: he offered model personal or family devotions for morning, evening, and at meals, and biblical summaries of God's calling in the church, society, and family and economic life.

> **Few figures in world history have been so celebrated five hundred years after their initial impact in the way that Luther is being celebrated at this time.**

These few words cannot hope to capture the dynamic of a gifted individual of towering emotions, deep theological insights, fierce critique of foes, incisive interpretation and proclamation of the biblical message. Few figures in world history have been so celebrated five hundred years after their initial impact in the way that Luther is being celebrated at this time. In recent years he has won attention as one of the most significant figures in German and world history. His posting of the theses on indulgences has been acclaimed as one of most critical turns in Western history ever.

What is his appeal in the twenty-first century? Why is anyone interested? Because Martin Luther's proclamation of the rescue and restoration of sinners by God's own becoming human, dying, and rising as Jesus of Nazareth still echoes into twenty-first-century ears and hearts!

Katharina von Bora Luther, Mother of the Lutheran Reformation

Kirsi Stjerna

Katharina von Bora Luther is the most famous of the Reformation era matriarchs. She established herself as Martin Luther's equal and "partner in calamities" and excelled as the manager of their large household and family affairs. A pioneer in many ways as a first-generation Protestant woman, Katharina was among the first women who married a priest; she set a model for Lutheran parsonage life. She embodied the Reformation teachings of the holiness of family life and spousal love, and of the godliness of the daily vocation of parenting.

Katharina was born in 1499 to an impoverished noble family. At the age of five she was placed in the care of Benedictine sisters in Brehna. Such practice was not uncommon among noble families, and girls could greatly benefit from convent education and shelter. A few years later, Katharina moved with two of her aunts to a more ascetically oriented Cistercian convent in Nimbschen, where she took her vows as a nun at the age of sixteen. In the convent she learned to read and write some Latin, study the scriptures, and practice religious disciplines, just as she also achieved many life skills that later she would come to use with her duties as the reformer's spouse.

While we do not know of her dreams and aspirations, we can admire her courage with the risky choice of leaving her safe convent for an unknown future. She never spoke ill of her years with the sisters, but it is clear that she made an active choice to leave that lifestyle after reading Luther's writings, particularly his criticism of monastic life and celibacy. In a dramatic escape—with plans coordinated by Luther and executed by city counselor and merchant Leonard Koppe, who risked a death penalty for this action—Katharina left with eleven other sisters and eventually landed in Wittenberg.

This bust of Katharina von Bora Luther depicts the two faces of her life: humble young nun and mature confident woman. The bust is located in the small museum in the house in Torgau, Germany, where she died in 1552.

Life outside the monastery

While in Wittenberg, Katharina first lived at the house of Lucas Cranach, the famous painter, pharmacist, and real-estate mogul, where she learned about life outside the convent walls, including normal domestic duties. She fell in love with a young university student named Jerome Baumgartner, who, under family pressure, ended up marrying someone younger and richer. Luther witnessed Katharina's heartbreak and, panicking about the fate of the ex-nun with no family connections in town, he tried his best at matchmaking—to Katharina's annoyance.

Katharina herself saw no urgency to marry. It remains unclear what led Katharina and Martin Luther to marry. Perhaps in part for convenience, in part for conviction, the two wedded in the summer of 1525 in a small ceremony with just close friends present. The more public wedding party in town two weeks later attracted significant attention and slandering of the bride. Opponents predicted curses of all kind from this scandalous coupling of two ex-monastics.

Katharina and Luther found themselves deeply in love with each other.

> **"**
> *In Luther's own words, Katharina taught the theologian about God's love and care.*
> **"**

Luther called Katharina his "sweetheart" and "lord." She exercised unusual autonomy for a woman in her time. Caring for her eccentric and overbooked "partner in calamities" was a full-time job. In addition, she boarded students, housed a constant flow of visitors, raised farm animals, cultivated her abundant gardens, and brewed beer. She managed to increase the family's assets by purchasing land, such as her beloved orchard in Zullsdorf.

Katharina gave birth to six children: Johannes, Elisabeth, Magdalena, Martin Jr., Paul, and Margaretha. Two of her daughters died young; she also lost two children in miscarriages. In Luther's own words, Katharina taught the theologian about God's love and care. In their parenting, in joys and grief, the couple together learned about the saving faith.

Statue of Katharina von Bora located in the courtyard of the Lutherhaus in Wittenberg.

Katharina found her calling as the wife and mother in the Luther household. She left no autobiography, but her husband's letters portray her as a remarkable person: gifted, strong-willed, and capable in so many ways. If there is one word for Katharina, it would be "unflappable."

After Luther died, Katharina endured financial hardship that forced her to beg for help for her children. She had been named as Luther's heir in his will—a sign of her equality in marriage—but Saxon laws required her to have a male guardian. Luther's colleague and friend Philipp Melanchthon served in that role, with Katharina thus maintaining her independence in reality.

The widow died from injuries from falling off a wagon on her way out of plague-struck Wittenberg. On her deathbed she declared her faith: she was going to stick to Christ like a burr sticks to a fur coat. She is buried in Torgau.

For further reading

Kirsi Stjerna. *Women and the Reformation*. Oxford: Blackwell, 2008.

Philipp Melanchthon (1497–1560)

Timothy J. Wengert

Philipp Melanchthon was Martin Luther's closest colleague at the University of Wittenberg from 1518 until Luther's death in 1546. He was responsible for writing the Augsburg Confession, the most important witness by Lutherans to the Christian faith and still used by many churches today. His work in theology and biblical interpretation helped to shape the Lutheran testimony to the gospel during the Reformation.

In 1497 a child was born to Georg Schwartzerdt and Barbara Reuter in the Reuter family's house in the Bretten, in southwest Germany. His father, an armorer and artillery specialist for the Count Elector Philipp of the Palatinate, named him after his lord and even had the electoral astrologer cast the child's horoscope. Philipp was a prodigy, and after his father's untimely death his mother sent him to live with a relative by marriage, Elizabeth Reuchlin, in the nearby town of Pforzheim, where he attended the Latin school and quickly became proficient in Greek. When her brother, the famous scholar Johannes Reuchlin, came to visit, he was so impressed with the boy's knowledge that he gave him a Greek grammar, inscribing it with *Melan-chthon*, the Greek equivalent of Schwartzerdt ("black earth"). Like many trained in the humanities in that time, he used this Greek form of his name exclusively in the years to come.

Melanchthon received a bachelor of arts degree from the University of Heidelberg and a master of arts from the University of Tübingen. This degree gave him the right to teach in the arts faculty there. At the same time he was a copy editor at the printery of Thomas Anshelm, where he published his first works. When Johannes Reuchlin was approached in 1518 by the University of Wittenberg in Saxony about teaching Greek there, he recommended instead his relative Philipp, who by this time had become famous for his abilities in classical Greek. Melanchthon subsequently accepted the call and became the first professor of Greek at that relatively young institution. Upon his arrival, he gave an inaugural lecture to the entire university that (unlike his unassuming, small stature) impressed everyone, especially Martin Luther, who quickly became his mentor. The following year Melanchthon received, under Luther's guidance, the first degree in theology, the so-called bachelor of Bible, which allowed him to lecture on the content of the biblical message and not just the Greek text.

Becoming Luther's right-hand man

At this time, of course, Luther's case with Rome was Wittenberg's chief concern. Melanchthon's first textbook on rhetoric included praise for Reuchlin, Erasmus, *and* Luther, who was especially lauded for his theology. In the summer of 1519, Melanchthon accompanied Luther to Leipzig for the debates with Johann Eck, and it was reported that he supplied references to the church fathers for Luther's use there. His account of the debate was quickly printed and turned what was likely a technical defeat for Luther into public victory. In 1521, with Luther in protective custody in the Wartburg Castle, Melanchthon

> **"**
> *Melanchthon was responsible for writing the Augsburg Confession, the most important witness by Lutherans to the Christian faith and still used by many churches today.*
> **"**

published a set of lectures on major theological topics derived from Paul's Letter to the Romans (which to both Luther and Melanchthon contained the sum of Christian teaching) and titled it *Loci communes theologici* (theological commonplaces). He published several revised versions over his career.

With Luther's return to the university in March 1522, Melanchthon helped his older colleague prepare the German translation of the New Testament for publication in September. From 1523 to 1524 he was rector of the university. By 1527 both he and Luther had received special appointments (or chairs) that allowed them to teach whatever they wished. As a result, Melanchthon taught in both the arts and theology faculties, producing basic textbooks on Latin and Greek grammar, rhetoric, dialectics (logic), and history for the arts and commentaries on Romans, Colossians, Proverbs, and some psalms (along with the *Loci communes*) for theology.

Because Luther was an outlaw of the Holy Roman Empire, Melanchthon was often called upon to represent Saxony at various diets (parliaments) and colloquies. Thus, in 1530, he was in Augsburg where he became the main drafter of the Augsburg Confession, even now the chief confession of faith for Lutherans around the world. The following year he published a defense (Latin: *Apologia*) of the Augsburg Con-

This statue of Philipp Melanchthon stands in the marketplace in front of the town hall in Wittenberg, Germany. Psalm 119:46 is engraved on the base of the statue: "I will also speak of your decrees before kings, and shall not be put to shame."

fession. Together these became the most important expositions of Wittenberg's faith and were subsequently subscribed to by many theologians of that time and ours. In 1536 he worked with the Strasbourg reformer Martin Bucer in establishing what was called the Wittenberg Concord among many of the parties that had been in disagreement over Christ's presence in the Lord's supper since the mid-1520s. In 1541 Melanchthon participated in the Regensburg Colloquy against his old nemesis Johann Eck. Although those discussions yielded a temporary agreement on the doctrine of justification, they collapsed over the question of the nature of the church and its authority.

Expanding on Luther's theology

After Luther's death in 1546, many viewed Melanchthon as the most important evangelical (Lutheran) theologian. However, disputes over certain church practices (adiaphora), the bondage of the will, justification by faith, and the Lord's supper tarnished his reputation among some later Lutherans. Nevertheless, many of his theological methods and insights became ensconced in the *Formula of Concord*, a 1576 Lutheran confession composed by the second generation of Lutheran reformers and responsible for the survival of a specifically Lutheran witness to the gospel in German-speaking lands.

Melanchthon's theology especially emphasized the relation between law (which maintains civil order and restrains evil in this world and terrifies the conscience before God) and gospel (through which God comforts the terrified). He also gleaned from Luther the proper distinction between human righteousness (which suffices for relations in this world and includes a certain level of human freedom) and divine righteousness (announced to the sinner as the forgiveness of sin through Christ's death and resurrection, which cannot be earned by human works or effort). On the Lord's supper, Melanchthon emphasized the difference between the Lutheran position and the Roman Catholic notions of sacrifice and of Christ's presence outside the action of the meal, while at the same time insisting on Christ's presence in the meal *with* the bread and wine (the language of the Wittenberg Concord).

In April 1560, Melanchthon came down with a severe cold brought on during his trip from Leipzig to Wittenberg in a rainstorm. According to his son-in-law, Caspar Peucer, who was at his bedside, his last words were from Romans 8:31, "If God is for us, who is against us?"—words that remain a fitting summary of his life and teaching.

For further reading

Gregory B. Graybill. *The Honeycomb Scroll: Philipp Melanchthon at the Dawn of the Reformation*. Minneapolis: Fortress Press, 2015.

Clyde Manschreck. *Melanchthon: The Quiet Reformer*. Nashville: Abingdon, 1958.

Johannes Bugenhagen (1485–1558)

Martin Lohrmann

Many best-selling books continue to promote the importance of organizing our lives, both individually and socially. Being organized can help us free up physical space and mental space; it can help us focus on what is really important instead of constantly cleaning up messes.

On this point, the Lutheran Reformation was blessed to have a fantastic organizer: Luther's colleague Johannes Bugenhagen. Alongside Luther and Melanchthon, Bugenhagen was a master of putting faith into action.

Even before he came to Wittenberg, Bugenhagen was a priest and teacher who cared about finding meaningful ways to live out Christian faith. Once he read Luther's great book about faith and service, *The Freedom of a Christian* (1520), he knew he had found a theological home. At age thirty-five he left his native Pomerania (present-day Poland) and moved to Wittenberg to learn more. In the years that followed he became a teacher at the university, head pastor of the City Church, and general superintendent (a Lutheran bishop) for the region.

> **"**
> *Bugenhagen was a master of putting faith into action.*
> **"**

With a strong knowledge of the Bible and of theologians like St. Augustine, Bugenhagen wrote many biblical commentaries and theological tracts. Of these, one of his most significant is a letter to the people of Hamburg

Statue of Johannes Bugenhagen located in Wittenberg.

on the right relationship between faith and good works (recently translated into English by Kurt K. Hendel, in Johannes Bugenhagen, *Selected Writings,* vol. 1 [Minneapolis: Fortress Press, 2015]).

How do we live out our faith?

For Bugenhagen as for Luther, the freedom that comes from faith in Christ provides the starting point for true good works that serve neighbors with no strings attached. To use an image from contemporary science, we might say that faith and good works are the double helix of a Christian life: like strands of DNA they are both separate and intimately connected.

In addition to the gospel at work in individuals, how does faith get lived out in communities? How do these values translate into beneficial structures that serve daily life? If people are saved by faith alone, why might "establishment" things like social institutions and church structures even matter?

This is where Bugenhagen's skills as an organizer shine. He wrote several "church orders," Reformation church constitutions for cities and territories. Over his career, he wrote or helped write church orders for such cities as Braunschweig, Hamburg, and Lübeck and for lands such as Denmark and Pomerania.

These church orders begin with statements of faith in Christ. After basing reconciliation on God's grace alone, Bugenhagen's orders then make arrangements for how to build people up spiritually and physically by offering gospel-centered worship, supporting schools, and providing social services like relief for the poor and health care. Church orders also describe how to collect funds for these projects and make sure they are carried out in responsible, accountable ways.

Practical matters like these were not just details or afterthoughts for the reformers. Good theology serves daily life and transforms real lives and communities. Finding ways to support such strong gospel-centered communities was a major goal of Bugenhagen's work as a church organizer.

In this way, Bugenhagen gave the church a strong "how to" legacy when it came to sharing faith and serving the common good. He is an example of the blessings that can come through grace-based organizing.

The Lutheran Reformation Goes Global

L. DeAne Lagerquist

When Christopher Columbus set sail to find a sea route to India the vast majority of Europeans were Christians, most of the world's Christians lived in Europe, and Martin Luther was a ten-year-old school boy. During Luther's lifetime and throughout the sixteenth century, Europe and Christianity both changed a great deal. The ferment of religious reform spread across the continent producing a variety of churches that often aligned with political trends and the emergence of nations. By the mid-seventeenth century Lutheranism was consolidated in northern German territories, Scandinavia, and the Baltic. Even before Luther arrived in Wittenberg in 1508, Europeans were launching commercial ventures, establishing colonies, and sending missionaries around the globe. At the Diet of Augsburg in 1530, there was a native American in Emperor Charles's entourage. A century later Swedish Lutherans migrated to North America, making their homes along the Delaware River. Immigrants from European Lutheran areas planted churches wherever they settled during the eighteenth and nineteenth centuries. By the early eighteenth century Lutheran missionaries began the work that would generate new Lutheran churches in every hemisphere. Five centuries after Luther, Lutheranism is an international movement. As is true of Christianity more generally, the most rapid expansion now is in the Southern Hemisphere. In 2016, the growing membership of the Ethiopian Evangelical Church Mekane Yesus (6.4 million) is nearly equal to that of the Church of Sweden (6.5 million).

A signpost in the courtyard of Mission Eine Welt ("Mission One World") in Neuen-dettelsau, Germany, shows the direction and distance to many of the locations where missionaries were sent from Neuendettelsau beginning in the mid-nineteenth century.

In the earliest years of the Reformation, students from various parts of Europe, such as the Swedish brothers Olavus and Laurentius Petri, were attracted to the University of Wittenberg, where they were inspired by Luther and his colleagues. Although the specific situation in their home churches differed from that in Saxony, the seeds these theologians brought back with them bore fruit in local reformations. As in German territories, the spread of Lutheranism into Scandinavia, the Baltic, and eastern Europe coincided with the development of the evangelical movement. It was most successful where the close association between church and civil authorities (the so-called Constantinianism of the Holy Roman Empire) was continued, though on a smaller scale than previously. The territorial principle—the one who rules is responsible for the religion of those who are ruled—was established by the Peace of Augsburg in 1555. The result was that well into the twentieth century most European Lutherans lived in nations where the majority of citizens were Lutheran and where national culture was intimately intertwined with Lutheran theology and practice. When theologians' concerns for evangelical reform overlapped with others' political interests, it was possible to put new church orders and religious practices in place by legal action. Changes in church members' own convictions and piety followed, likely more gradually. Along with liturgical modifications, translations of the Bible and key theological documents into local languages were significant tools for fostering that change. Where evangelical reform and Lutheran theology failed to gain political support, as in England, or encountered strong Catholic opposition, as in Austria and Poland, Lutheranism either faded or developed as a minority tradition, although still within a Christian majority.

Different reasons for reform

In the area that now comprises the five Nordic nations, the impulse for reform was generated more by commercial and educational contact with German influences than as a response to abuses within the church. Because the theological disputes that occupied German Lutherans were less pronounced in these churches, the Augsburg Confession and Luther's Small Catechism, rather than the entire Book of Concord, were given primary authority. After the breakup of the Kalmar Union in 1523, the Swedish monarch ruled Finland and the Danish monarch ruled both Norway and Iceland. Their support for reform was mixed with their political interests and shifting power relations with nobility. Church leaders took responsibility for specifics such as the Community Chest (see "Luther on Worship and Welfare," page 115), instruction in Luther's Small Catechism, and vernacular sermons. After Christian III established Lutheranism within his realm in 1536, Johannes Bugenhagen helped to revise the Danish church order along the Wittenberg model. Reform was imposed in Norway and Iceland, where resistance was fueled more by anti-Danish sentiment than by theological disagreement. Rather like English monarchs, Swedish kings vacillated in their religious leanings, some toward Calvinism, others toward Catholicism. In 1593, the church assembly in Uppsala made the Augsburg Confession normative for the Swedish church. Under Gustavus Adolphus's command, the Swedish army supported the Protestant cause in the Thirty Years' War, resolved by the Peace of Westphalia, which reaffirmed territorialism in 1648.

Lutherans in the Western Hemisphere

Already in the sixteenth century, lone Lutherans traveled beyond Europe; however, the founding of Lutheran congregations in the Americas, South Africa, and Australia began only when groups of Lutherans migrated to those areas and established communities. Among the earliest was Frederick Lutheran Church, organized in 1666 in the Danish colony of Charlotte Amalie, on St. Thomas, Virgin Islands. Very few other Lutherans found themselves in places where the government supported their church. Most often Lutheran immigrants were attracted to areas where they could improve their material circumstances, but where they did not speak the common language and their religion was a minority among Roman Catholics or other Protestants. Without support from their home churches, and regarded as foreigners, they confronted significant challenges. Everywhere they faced limited financial resources, clerical shortage, and difficulties retaining members. As they adapted to unfamiliar customs, they also established institutions, developed organized mechanisms for cooperation, and produced common worship materials suitable for their new setting. Unfortunately, the complexity of immigrant Lutheran churches' institutional histories sometimes overwhelms the stories of their members. In each place the particulars varied, but there were recognizable patterns.

Whatever their motives for leaving Europe, the characteristic theology and practices Lutherans carried with them influenced the congregations and church bodies they founded in their new homes. Most came from places where they were the majority, but a few did not. In the 1730s the Catholic Prince-Archbishop of Salzburg expelled thousands of Lutherans, some of whom established New Ebenezer in colonial Georgia. In the nineteenth century the recently independent Brazilian government recruited Lutherans from the Rhine River valley to populate Rio Grande do Sul; similarly, American railroad companies offered affordable farmland in the Midwest. The Scandinavians who responded brought a piety shaped by recent awakenings. Rejecting the Prussian Union of 1817, Saxon Lutherans traveled to Perry County, Missouri, and to Australia, where they organized churches characterized by strict confessionalism. After gathering congregations, a typical next step was to seek pastors from Europe, as did members of the German business community in Buenos Aires, Argentina, in the 1840s. Before long, Lutherans linked congregations into synods and set up institutions to meet their members' needs: schools, hospitals, and agencies to provide other social services. In Brazil these institutions were modeled on those in Bethel and benefited from the work of deaconesses from Kaiserswerth, Germany. Each church's colleges and seminaries began to prepare native-born leaders who were more at home in the culture than those imported from the old country. This became increasingly important in the late nineteenth and early twentieth centuries when subsequent generations preferred the local language: English, Spanish, or Portuguese. As the churches matured, they also began to cooperate across synodical boundaries defined by old confessional and ethnic identities. The Common Service (1888) developed in the United States resulted from such collaboration. Both the Evangelical Lutheran Church in Canada (1986) and the Evangelical Lutheran Church in America (1988) were formed by a series of such mergers. Formed in 1949, the Evangelical Church of the Lutheran Confession in Brazil brought together several bodies. It has cooperated with the smaller Evangelical Lutheran Church of Brazil to publish a fifteen-volume translation of Luther's works in Portuguese.

Expanding throughout the globe

Most of the Lutheran churches in Asia and Africa and in South and Central America grew from Lutheran missions undertaken since the early eighteenth century. Preoccupied with reforming the church close by, Luther's generation made no efforts to evangelize beyond Europe. Theologians of following generations (the period known as Lutheran Orthodoxy) posited that the gospel had been preached to the whole world during the apostolic age and so took no responsibility for that task. The few mission efforts in these centuries were isolated and short-lived.

Sustained missionary work was activated by Pietists' dual concern for personal spirituality and holistic service. The earliest foreign missionaries were trained and supervised by the Francke Foundation in Halle, Germany. Notable among them was Bartholomäus Ziegenbalg, who was sent by Frederick IV to the native residents of Tranquebar, a Danish commercial colony in south India, in 1706. Most other Lutheran missionaries, however, worked in areas not ruled by their own national governments and were supported by voluntary societies rather than royal patronage. At one point there were more than eighty such groups in Scandinavia. Some focused their work on a particular group of people or a region, while others, such as the Berlin Mission Society, sponsored missions in several locations. Support from women's organizations was both spiritual and material. Lutheran missions had expanded to several areas of Africa, China, Papua New Guinea, Indonesia, Jerusalem, and Puerto Rico by the end of the nineteenth century and into Latin America by the middle of the twentieth. Missionaries founded congregations and institutions that reflected their particular sort of Lutheranism and their approach to local culture. Although some missionaries cooperated across these differences, the variety of their nationalities and church sponsors contributed to the formation of several Lutheran bodies in some countries.

Consistent with Pietist views, the earliest Lutheran missionaries aimed to foster personal experiences of conversion. In each setting they considered how to translate the gospel for the new audience. Founding churches followed. Ziegenbalg's methods set a model for this work. Preaching required learning the language and customs, often with the help of locals. As quickly as possible, the Bible and the Small Catechism were translated. Like their Reformation-era forebears, missionaries opened schools and tended to peoples' well-being. With the newly converted they determined how to respond to local customs. Working in Sumatra in the late nineteenth century, Ludwig Nommensen generally accommodated Batak

> **What began as an evangelical movement to reform the Roman Catholic Church has become a family of churches, no longer confined to Europe.**

customs but rejected ancestor worship. Lutherans in India were divided by their attitudes toward caste distinctions within the church; the Arcot Lutheran Church was formed in 1863 by those firmly opposed. Founded in the 1930s, the Tao Fong Shan mission to Buddhists in Hong Kong adopted a vegetarian diet and used Chinese architecture for its buildings. Development of local leadership and autonomous organization was generally slow. Aaron, the first Tamil Lutheran pastor, was ordained in 1733, a quarter century after the Tranquebar mission began. Restrictions on missionary activity, particularly by Germans, during two world wars accelerated the transition to self-governing churches starting in the early twentieth century.

Shaped by local concerns

Preparation of indigenous worship resources and practices has been a similarly gradual process. Old styles and translated hymns continue in use alongside newly created liturgies and music which now enliven congregations around the world. Similarly, theologians from these churches are advancing Lutheran reflection upon and articulation of the gospel and giving leadership to Lutherans' work on behalf of neighbor and the world. Latin Americans, such as Bishop Medardo Gomez of El Salvador and Brazilian theologian Vitor Westhelle, point out the connections between spiritual justification and social justice. African Lutherans, following the insights of martyred Ethiopian Gudina Tumsa, emphasize the holistic implications of the gospel. Lutherans across Asia engage in interfaith dialogue with their neighbors.

Much has changed since the sixteenth century. What began as an evangelical movement to reform the Roman Catholic Church has become a family of churches, no longer confined to Europe. The names of the church bodies are noteworthy: many of them include the title of Lutheran, others use the name Evangelical (spreading the gospel), and some names declare their adherence to the Augsburg Confession. Lutherans associate with one another through the Lutheran World Federation (with 72 million congregants in 145 church bodies in 98 nations) or the International Lutheran Council (with 3 million congregants in 35 member bodies in more than 30 nations). Although they now use many more languages, twenty-first-century Lutherans still teach the centrality of grace, and their churches are still identified by their commitment to word and sacrament.

Lutherans in North America

Mark Granquist

Lutherans have been in North America for almost four hundred years, beginning with an ill-fated Danish expedition to explore the Arctic in 1619. Scandinavian colonization efforts led to the first two permanent Lutheran communities, a Swedish colony on the Delaware River from 1638 and a Danish colony on the Virgin Islands from 1672, but neither was a major settlement. There were a number of Lutherans in the Dutch colony in New York in the seventeenth century, and they formed a parish there in 1649. It's the oldest surviving Lutheran congregation in the United States. Increasing migration of Germans to the middle colonies of Pennsylvania, Maryland, and New Jersey in the eighteenth century brought the formation of scattered Lutheran congregations in the region, while Lutheran refugees from European wars settled in New York and Georgia. But those congregations were poor and mostly without pastoral leadership, as it was difficult to get Lutheran pastors to leave their comfortable European parishes to come to the wilds of North America. At times, colonial Lutheran congregations were plagued by failed pastors from Europe, or even outright imposters.

This situation improved in 1742 with the arrival of Pastor Henry Melchior Muhlenberg, sent to Pennsylvania by the Pietist Halle Institution in Germany. Muhlenberg quickly began to gather together the scattered Lutheran pastors and congregations into the first Lutheran synod, the Ministerium of Pennsylvania, formed in 1748. The Ministerium examined and regulated pastors, helped resolve disputes, and helped defend Lutheran congregations from the encroachments of other denominations. Through his personal leadership, Muhlenberg became the acknowledged leader of Lutherans in colonial America, which grew to about twenty-five thousand persons by 1790. A network of Lutheran congregations stretched from Georgia to New York, with the largest concentration in Pennsylvania, mostly worshiping in German. There was also a small German Lutheran settlement in Maine and one in the Canadian province of Nova Scotia.

Monument to Henry Melchior Muhlenberg located at The Lutheran Theological Seminary at Philadelphia.

Lutherans become Americans

With the coming of the American Revolutionary War (1775–83), Lutherans were caught up in the conflict. Some Lutherans remained neutral in the struggle, seeing it as an "English" problem. Other Lutherans supported the Revolution and served with distinction in the American forces, a few rising to positions of leadership. A smaller group remained loyal to the British crown, and some of them migrated to Ontario after the war. With the peace in 1783, Americans began to move west, seeking new lands in Appalachia and the Ohio River Valley. Lutherans streamed westward too, depleting established congregations in the East. This was a huge problem, for the lack of pastors, poor transportation, and immense distances meant that frontier Lutherans might go years without visits from a handful of traveling Lutheran missionaries. Slowly new congregations were formed on the frontier. The distances also necessitated the formation of new regional synods, first in New York, and then in Ohio, Virginia, Maryland, and the Carolinas.

Another struggle for these Lutherans was the conflict over the transition to using the English language. Most colonial Lutherans practiced their religion in German, but the younger generations, increasingly proficient in English, began to urge the use of that language in worship. The struggle over this was intense in the 1790s and 1800s, but inevitably the transition occurred. Lutherans learned to worship and do their theology in English and became more influenced by the English-speaking religious groups around them. The increasing number of regional Lutheran synods meant the need for a national organization, leading to the formation of the General Synod in 1820. This group existed to coordinate the work of the synods, and in 1826 formed the first Lutheran seminary, at Gettysburg, to address the extreme need for Lutheran pastors.

In the nineteenth century, these colonial or "Muhlenberg" Lutherans expanded across America and became involved with the growth of Protestant Christianity in the new country. This was a time of religious renewal and revivalism, and American Lutherans participated in these movements, which led to questions about Lutheran identity and practice, especially concerning its core documents, the Lutheran confessional writings. Some Lutherans sought to become more like their Protestant neighbors and to minimize Lutheran theological distinctiveness. Others sought a renewed appreciation for particularly Lutheran theology and worship, leading to conflict. Lutherans were also drawn into the national battle over slavery, with southern Lutherans defending the practice, while some northern Lutherans became increasingly opposed to it. During the Civil War southern Lutherans broke off from the General Synod, and in 1867 the northern Lutherans split over theological issues and formed a new group, the General Council.

Immigrants swell the ranks

Beginning in the 1840s a great wave of immigration from Europe to the United States began, and by 1918 some thirty million persons had crossed the Atlantic to North America. Lutherans were well represented in this migration, mainly from Germany and Scandinavia, but also from Lutheran areas in eastern Europe. Wanting to use the language of their homelands, and suspicious of the older, English-speaking "American" Lutherans, these new immigrants developed their own congregations and denominations rather than joining existing ones. Thus began the multiplication of Lutheran denominations in North America during the nineteenth century, and by 1900 there were at least twelve major groups and many smaller ones. Some of the differences involved language; there were German, Norwegian, Swedish, Danish, Finnish, Icelandic, and Slovak groups. But differences over theology and practice within each ethnic group led to even more denominational splintering. The largest of these groups was the German-language Missouri Synod, but all these new immigrant Lutheran denominations grew rapidly, and by 1900 Lutherans were the third-largest Protestant "family" in the United States, after the Baptists and Methodists.

For many new immigrants, their Lutheran congregations were the center of their religious, ethnic, and cultural lives. The congregations functioned in many roles, including assisting the new immigrants in their transition to American life. But the religious transition to this new country was difficult. In Europe religious life was provided (and determined) by the state; it was a given. In the United States, religion was voluntary, and if they wanted religious life the immigrants had to organize it (and pay for it!) themselves. The immigrants were poor, and there were never enough pastors; many immigrants took the freedom of religion as an opportunity to join non-Lutheran congregations or as an excuse to drop religion altogether. Only a fraction of Lutheran immigrants actually joined American Lutheran congregations.

> **By 1900 Lutherans were the third-largest Protestant 'family' in the United States, after the Baptists and Methodists.**

Despite all this, American Lutherans in the nineteenth century developed a rich world of congregations and institutions, including many schools, colleges, and seminaries, and social service institutions, including hospitals, orphanages, and retirement homes. The local congregations were often supported primarily by the women, who organized women's missionary societies and religious organizations. Though these denominations were stretched to their limits just to reach the new immigrants, many of them also aspired to join the great Protestant crusade to evangelize the world. Some Lutherans felt called to mission work within America (with Native Americans and African Americans), others to missionary service to Asia and Africa; many others formed voluntary mission societies to raise funds to support these missions. Lutherans also published thousands of books and hundreds of religious newspapers intended to further the work of their particular Lutheran denominations and organizations.

Lutherans developed this rich religious culture mostly away from the mainstream of American life, but in the twentieth century events drew them more fully into this world. The First World War (1914–1918) was pivotal; anti-foreign attitudes brought a quick transition to the use of English, while drastic restrictions slowed immigration to a trickle. Now moving quickly to the use of English, there seemed less of a need for separate ethnic Lutheran denominations, so the long process of mergers and consolidations began. Beyond this, Lutherans learned to work cooperatively through the National Lutheran Council and the Synodical Conference. The heady economic expansion of the 1920s ended with the crash of 1929 and the subsequent Depression of the 1930s, which dramatically squeezed the mission and ministries of these denominations.

Expansion and decline

After the full mobilization of the Second World War (for the United States, 1941–45), the expansion of the 1950s allowed American Lutherans to spread into new areas of the country, especially the South and West. The "Baby Boom" (1946–64) swelled congregational membership, and hundreds of new congregations were formed, many in the new suburbs. American Lutheranism hit its statistical peak around 1965, with some nine million members. Further merger activity resulted in the formation of two large denominations, the American Lutheran Church (ALC) in 1960 and the Lutheran Church in America (LCA) in 1962. With the Lutheran Church–Missouri Synod (LCMS), these three bodies represented 95 percent of all Lutherans in America. The Canadian congregations of these groups separated and formed their own Canadian Lutheran denominations during this time period.

By the beginning of the 1960s American Lutheranism was generally fully integrated into the mainstream of American Protestant life, but this happened as the mainstream itself was beginning to decline. The 1960s was a turbulent period, with social and political tensions reaching a boiling point. Civil rights, the question of the war in Vietnam, and the push for women's rights all wracked the country and divided denominations and congregations. The ALC and LCA moved toward some of the new social realities; for example, they began to ordain women into the Lutheran ministry in 1970. The LCMS was divided internally over many of these issues and suffered dissension and division in the early 1970s, as a moderate group broke away to form the Association of Evangelical Lutheran Churches (AELC) in 1976.

Through the 1980s, the ALC, LCA, and AELC moved toward closer ties, as the theological and social gaps between them and the LCMS widened. In 1988 these three formed the Evangelical Lutheran Church in America (ELCA), which represented about two-thirds of American Lutherans, with the LCMS numbering most of the other third. The Wisconsin Evangelical Lutheran Synod (WELS) is the largest of a number of other much smaller Lutheran denominations. The decline of old-line Protestantism in America and the rise of Evangelical groups are reflected

> "
> *As Lutheranism moves toward its 500th anniversary, it is challenged to draw on these historical resources to meet the challenges ahead.*
> "

in the number of American Lutherans, which declined to about seven million by 2015. While the more conservative LMCS has lost a moderate number of members, the decline of the ELCA has been steeper, fueled by internal debates about ministry, ecumenism, and human sexuality. Two new Lutheran denominations have been formed by those leaving the ELCA, the Lutheran Congregations in Mission for Christ (LCMC) in 2001 and the North American Lutheran Church (NALC) in 2010.

Though buffeted by the events of the last fifty years, American Lutheranism remains an important religious family within the country. It has a strong and distinct tradition of theological and spiritual life, robust traditions of worship, important institutions of learning and social service, and thousands of active congregations. As Lutheranism moves toward its 500th anniversary, it is challenged to draw on these historical resources to meet the challenges ahead.

Twentieth-Century Profile: Dietrich Bonhoeffer

Gary M. Simpson

ietrich Bonhoeffer (1906–1945) was a German Lutheran pastor, theologian, and martyr who lived his adult life under the fascist Nazi regime of Adolf Hitler's Third Reich. Bonhoeffer had resisted the totalitarian tyranny of Nazism from its takeover of Germany beginning in January 1933, and on the radio he openly denounced Hitler's April 1933 Aryan Civil Service law, which had banned Jews from being German civil servants, and which eventually led to the murder of over six million European Jews. Bonhoeffer's resistance to Hitler grew throughout the 1930s, and he became an influential young leader of the Protestant "confessing church struggle" against the Nazification of German Protestantism. In July 1940 Bonhoeffer's brother-in-law, Hans von Dohnányi, convinced him to join a conspiracy group within Hitler's own military intelligence to assassinate Hitler. Bonhoeffer became a double agent. In April 1943 Bonhoeffer was arrested, imprisoned, and interrogated. Two years later Hitler personally gave the order to execute Bonhoeffer along with other conspirators, which was carried out at Flossenbürg Prison on April 9, 1945, just two weeks before the Allied forces entered Berlin.

Bonhoeffer had been raised in an aristocratic and intellectual family and studied theology at the University of Berlin, where his father was a professor of psychiatry. He was a gifted student and at the age of twenty-one he finished his first doctoral dissertation, *Sanctorum Communio*, on the proposition of "Christ existing as church-community" by probing and

Memorial stone at the Flossenbürg concentration camp marking the spot where Dietrich Bonhoeffer and other members of the resistance were executed on April 9, 1945. The plaque reads, "In resistance to dictator and terror [these people] gave their lives for freedom, justice, and human dignity."

building upon Martin Luther's Christ-centered approach to the communion of saints. Three years later Bonhoeffer finished his second dissertation, a German requirement for future professors. In 1930 he went to New York City on a scholarship for a year at Union Theological Seminary, where he studied with well-known theologians, including Reinhold Niebuhr, the most famous American Christian social ethicist of the time. During that year, he regularly worshiped and participated in numerous ways at the renowned Abyssinian Baptist Church in Harlem. There he gained firsthand knowledge of the systematic racist discrimination against African Americans, of their black theology and deep spirituality, and of the Harlem Renaissance.

Bonhoeffer had come to the United States with the common German-Lutheran conviction that Christian faith and theology had little interest in concrete political life. After returning to Germany he soon became a young leader within the growing ecumenical movement of the day. He also became a strong voice within the various ecumenical peace movements across Europe, making many friends and especially establishing close ties with influential church leaders in England. These friendships and ties made him a valuable double agent who could communicate with the Allied forces about the conspiracy to assassinate Hitler and the plans to set up an alternative German government that would negotiate peace with the Allied powers, plans which of course did not come to fruition.

Addressing uncomfortable realities

Between 1935 and 1939 Bonhoeffer became an even more integral part of the "Confessing Church" and the "Church Struggle." The Confessing Church, which existed outside the normal German Protestant church structures, started its own preachers' seminary, first in Zingst on the Baltic Sea and eventually on the Finkenwalde estate near the Baltic seaport of Stettin. The Confessing Church appointed Bonhoeffer as the director and teacher of the Finkenwalde seminary. Finkenwalde was the setting that inspired some of Bonhoeffer's most famous writings: *Discipleship*, *Life Together*, and *Prayerbook of the Bible: An Introduction to the Psalms*. He took key notions from his first dissertation, *Sanctorum Communio*, and developed them for more popular audiences. Among these key notions is that Jesus lived and acted

Bust of Dietrich Bonhoeffer from the chapel on the grounds of the Flossenbürg concentration camp, where Bonhoeffer was executed in 1945.

> **"**
> **'As Christ bears our burdens, so we are to bear the burden of our sisters and brothers.'**
> **"**

vicariously with and for human beings and that Jesus' incarnate, crucified, and risen way of life forms the way of life of his disciples. As Bonhoeffer puts it in *Discipleship*: In Christ "God is a God who bears. . . . Bearing constitutes being a Christian. . . . As Christ bears our burdens, so we are to bear the burden of our sisters and brothers."

Bonhoeffer's core theological convictions shaped his later writings as he attempted to address new circumstances. For instance, he was trying in the thirteen manuscripts in his *Ethics*—we have only draft, not completed, chapters—to construct a "concrete Christian ethic" both for times out of joint and for more ordinary times. In his oft-read *Letters and Paper from Prison* he brings his core Christian convictions into conversation with a "religionless Christianity" and with a "world come of age." In "After Ten Years," his 1942 Christmas letter to his family and fellow conspirators, he notes that following a "God who bears" leads to "an experience of incomparable value that we have for once learned to see the great events of world history from below, from the perspective of the outcast, the suspects, the maltreated, the powerless, the oppressed and reviled, in short from the perspective of the suffering."

Twenty-First Century Profile: Leymah Gbowee

Elizabeth Hunter

"**G**od is calling us today to reclaim our space," Leymah Gbowee, a Lutheran peacemaker and modern-day reformer from Liberia told the almost two thousand women at the 2011 Women of the ELCA Triennial Gathering.

Gbowee, a mother of six who won a Nobel Peace Prize that same year, knows all about reclaiming space. Growing up, she had a comfortable upbringing, thanks to hard-working parents who had weathered political instability in years past. In 1990, when she was seventeen and a new college student, civil war forced Gbowee and her family to flee from their home and take refuge at the guest compound of St. Peter's Lutheran Church in Monrovia, Liberia. Terrified, the teen prayed for God to end the war and listened to her mother tell funny stories to try to lift their spirits over the sounds of shooting and executions outside St. Peter's walls.

One Sunday soldiers came for the people in the church. One of the soldiers, a commander, warned her family to leave before the next group of fighters came. They did, moving across the boulevard to her sister's boyfriend's apartment.

Leymah Gbowee, Nobel Peace laureate, speaks during a press conference at Eastern Mennonite University, Harrisonburg, Virginia (October 14, 2011).

That night, a different group of soldiers entered the church and massacred those who had sheltered at the church. Gbowee and her family had barely escaped with their lives.

During the war, she began doing volunteer social work for nearly five difficult years through the Lutheran Church in Liberia/Lutheran World Federation's Trauma Healing and Reconciliation Program, helping ex-combatants and others to recover from the trauma of war. It was a life-changing experience of peace-building.

Consider: Where might you and others in your community need to constructively interfere in a community, town, state, or country? Human trafficking? Unemployment? Advocating for an end to racial disparities in justice? Do you need to reclaim a particular space? A corner where drugs are sold or women and children are trafficked? A series of abandoned properties that could be turned into community space or a playground?

Later, working and praying together, she and thousands of other Christian and Muslim women in Liberia used nonviolent methods to reclaim their country and end Liberia's long-running civil war. Gbowee and other women stood between warlords and armies, toppling a corrupt regime and bringing about peace in 2003.

Teachings for Western Lutherans

When women see a problem—not just a war, but someone caught in domestic violence, someone suffering from addiction—women can do something, Gbowee told Triennial participants that day, adding: "Faith without action is dead" (James 2:26).

After acting to resolve a situation, bold women don't stop. They simply continue their "constructive interference," she said.

> **"**
> *'The God we serve is not a God of halfway [but] a God of wholeness.'*
> **"**

After peace came to Liberia, women continued "interfering" to ensure the rights of women. They spoke out against corruption, spoke up in cases of rape, and registered thousands of women to vote in an election that resulted in the country's first female president, Ellen Johnson

Fun fact: Gbowee is the second Lutheran woman to win the Nobel Peace Prize. In 1982, Alva Myrdal, a member of the Church of Sweden, was the first Lutheran woman to win the prize. Other Lutheran Nobel Peace Prize winners are Albert Schweitzer (1952), Dag Hammarskjöld (1961), and Norman Borlaug (1970).

Sirleaf. They provided support and assistance when women in other countries—Ivory Coast and Democratic Republic of Congo—chose to stand up for peace.

"The God we serve is not a God of halfway [but] a God of wholeness," Gbowee said. God calls us to go beyond what we're comfortable with, and enter into the places that need reclaiming, the spaces God has given us. She assured her listeners, "[God] who called you will equip you."

Worship and the Arts

The Augsburg Confession, written in 1530 as a statement of faith for the Lutheran movement, defines the church as the assembly where the word of God is rightly preached and where the sacraments are administered in accordance with God's word. The Augsburg Confession further describes word and sacraments as "means of grace," through which the Holy Spirit works faith when and where it pleases God. "Church," therefore, is not something we do (and certainly not something we "have" to do). Church is what God is doing among and for and through us. We worship to hear with our ears the good news of God's love and forgiveness for us through Jesus Christ. We worship to be touched, bodily, with the water and the bread and wine of God's promise. And we worship to respond to this gift and promise with our prayers and praises.

The first three essays in this section invite us to consider worship and the sacraments of baptism and holy communion as central to our Christian identity. The remaining essays invite us to consider music and art as an expression of the faith—in two complementary ways. Music and art are time-honored ways in which Christians have expressed their faith in response to their awareness of God's presence and love. At the same time, Lutherans have been intentional about using the arts to communicate the biblical stories and the gospel message to those with eyes to see, ears to hear, and lips to sing. Martin Luther, himself an accomplished musician, used hymns to teach the faith. Johann Sebastian Bach's ability to convey the gospel through music is so powerful that he is often called the Fifth Evangelist. The visual arts, especially through the gifts of people like sixteenth-century painter, printer, and entrepreneur Lucas Cranach, were essential to reach a largely illiterate populace and still speak powerfully as nonverbal expressions of the faith.

Worship Matters

Kevin L. Strickland

What is worship and why does it matter?

Worship begins with the simple act of gathering. Woody Allen is quoted as saying, "Showing up is 80 percent of life." Yet worship doesn't start with our showing up. The pattern for worship in *Evangelical Lutheran Worship* gets the direction straight and ups the number: "The Holy Spirit calls us together as the people of God." Not 80 percent but 100 percent of the time. That is how Article 7 of the Augsburg Confession defines church: God calling us together around word and sacraments. God shows up, all the time! Because of what God does, we are church.

Elizabeth Eaton, presiding bishop of the Evangelical Lutheran Church in America, helps to center this church's mission in what it means to gather as a church together around word and sacraments. Bishop Eaton states, "When we gather for worship we hear God's word or promise. We confess our help-lessness and receive forgiveness. We pray and we welcome new brothers and sisters through baptism, promising to support them in their walk in faith. We are fed with the bread of life and receive our Lord poured out for us. And then we are sent back into the world. Worship is essential for the church's life and service." Worship is at the heart of what we do. There we find the cruci-fied Christ in risen form.

> But you are a chosen race, a royal priesthood, a holy nation, God's own people, in order that you may proclaim the mighty acts of him who called you out of darkness into his marvelous light. Once you

were not a people, but now you are God's people; once you had not received mercy, but now you have received mercy. (1 Peter 2:9-10)

Recently I have been involved in many conversations that have centered on "What does it mean to *be* the church?" "Being" church, for me, is embodying that verb in all we do and all we say. "Being" church, for me, offers an opportunity for each of us to remember that we are, as First Peter points out, called to proclaim (in word and deed) God's mighty acts.

Enjoying and sharing God's gifts

Every time we gather as God's people, we can gather around God's marvelous gifts of grace. Those gifts of grace nourish us so that we may point others to the mighty acts of God. Often in the church we become bogged down defining church by the numbers—numbers of decline in worship attendance, decline in giving, decline in _____ (fill in the blank)—and we forget to

 define church as we who have been called to point people to the life-changing, life-giving, and mighty acts of God, inviting others into this mission.

As the *Use of the Means of Grace: A Statement on the Practice of Word and Sacrament* points out, "In every celebration of the means of grace, God acts to show forth both the need of the world and the truth of the Gospel. In every gathering of Christians around the proclaimed Word and the holy sacraments, God acts to empower the Church for mission. Jesus Christ, who is God's living bread come down from heaven, has given his flesh to be the life of the world. This very flesh, given for the life of all, is encountered in the Word and sacraments" (Principle 51).

Within the ELCA, we gather in celebration of the means of grace every week in more than 9,600 congregations and do so with at least forty-one languages represented. Some assemblies gather around word and sacrament in beautiful sanctuaries ornately designed with stained glass windows and have a history of as many as two hundred years of ministry. Other assemblies gather in storefronts, bars, and coffee shops to proclaim Christ crucified and risen. Assemblies welcome refugees, provide ministry to the imprisoned, and offer reconciliation with welcome to those who would define themselves as unchurched or de-churched.

We are a church that includes in weekly worship a wide variety and array of music, cultural practices, and understandings of what "traditional" and "contemporary" look like. In worship we are church: gathered by God, every time. In worship we are Lutheran: hearing and proclaiming the story of salvation, law and gospel, the cross that raises us to life. We are together for it all, yet as we move toward and around the table, that togetherness becomes even more deep and wide, seen and unseen.

> There is a balm in Gilead to make the wounded whole;
> there is a balm in Gilead to heal the sin-sick soul. (ELW 614)

Worship becomes a "balm in Gilead," offering healing for whatever gives pain to our lives. It is a holy and awesome responsibility that we have been given in leading God's people in worship. Every week in countless assemblies, the body of Christ—the church—gathers. When we do, we assemble all of our wounds, our brokenness, our inequalities, our complacency, our lethargy, and our greatest moments of joy. We gather all of that together and we wash in a bath of forgiveness, dine at a table of mercy, and are fed with words of grace. When we leave worship, we don't leave the same. We have been changed to offer balm for a world in need.

Fed for the journey

Presiding Bishop Eaton has said, "Most of all we should come to worship expecting to be changed. We are touching, tasting, feeling, hearing, and seeing the one who knows us and loves us completely. Our lives are restored. We are set free. Fed for the journey, we are set loose to go in peace and serve the Lord. Thanks be to God."

Our pattern for worship ends with the Sending. Or does it? *The Sunday Assembly* includes a simple diagram that shows the fourfold pattern of Gathering, Word, Meal, and Sending as a never-ending cycle, continuously repeated.

Gordon Lathrop writes, "Sending is . . . *movement*: from the communion table to the cross in the world . . . the life cycle continues. The ending inevitably leads again to the gathering."

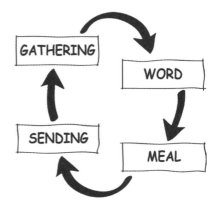

When we say, "Go in peace, serve the Lord," does our worship end? Worship is work that is never completely done. After we are fed and nourished by God's word and by bread and wine, we don't settle in for a long nap. We are not the same people who gathered. We have been formed again, re-membered as Christ's body, and are ready to be sent into the world God loves.

A prayer for after worship in *Evangelical Lutheran Worship* says:

> Grant, O Lord Jesus, that the ears which have heard the voice of your songs may be closed to the voice of dispute; that the eyes which have seen your great love may also behold your blessed hope; that the tongues which have sung your praise may speak the truth in love; that the feet which have walked in your courts may walk in the region of light; and that the bodies which have received your living body be restored in newness of life. Glory to you for your inexpressible gift; for you live and reign with the Father and the Holy Spirit, one God, now and forever. Amen. [*ELW*, p. 73]

May it be so!

'I Am Baptized!'

Scott A. Moore

Millions of Christians around the world identify with Martin Luther, the sixteenth-century theologian, priest, biblical scholar, professor, prolific writer, and church reformer. Many of these Christians call themselves Lutherans, a name that would be problematic for the former Augustinian friar, who said he did not want people to embrace his name and be called Lutherans but instead be called Christians. It is in Christ that Martin Luther repeatedly sought his own identity and where he hoped all Christians would find theirs. This identity is rooted clearly and profoundly in holy baptism. For Luther, baptism is the most precious gift that could have been given to the church, and it is in baptism that all the promises of God can be found.

Baptizatus sum. That's Latin for "I am baptized." If Luther were a young person today looking for the perfect tattoo to express his personal motto, it would likely be some form of "I am baptized." The importance of baptism was so clear for Luther that this phrase is considered his mantra, used whenever he was feeling his own mortality or needing God's assurances. It is such a small phrase, yet it is full of promise and hope and loaded with a theology so deep it would take a lifetime to explore.

Baptism is one of the moments when an individual encounters the love and grace of God and receives the gift of faith that makes all things right: right between us and God, right within ourselves, and right between us and the world. Baptism is not an accidental or random encounter. It is an intentional and clearly marked event where we come to know God's word of promise as it comes together with some simple water to make a most holy happening.

This "holy happening" of baptism is a divine encounter that we experience on many levels. It is also something we grow to understand over time, and that understanding is never really complete. A ninety-year-old "understands" the gifts of baptism differently than a nine-year-old child. God works through baptism to join us to Christ in profound ways, no matter our stage of life and regardless of our cognitive abilities. There isn't an age of reason necessary to be able to "get it." In baptism, we are joined to Christ's death and resurrection. As the words of the baptismal formula are spoken and the water makes our body wet, we die and we rise. Just as Christ died and was raised again, our holy bath drowns us and draws us into a new life. We are changed. We are made one with Christ forever. Whatever it is about our frail humanity that separates us from God, that which we call sin, it is overcome, and we are joined again to the divine humanity of Jesus Christ. We are united with Christ and given the gifts of the Holy Spirit.

> **For Luther, baptism is the most precious gift that could have been given to the church, and it is in baptism that all the promises of God can be found.**

Faith planted and nurtured

In baptism, the seeds of faith are planted in us and watered. Ideally, this faith is nurtured in a community of believers and grows throughout our lives, sometimes steadily, often in fits and starts. Some of us even come to the waters of baptism later in life with stories and experiences preparing us for that moment. Many in our tradition, however, are baptized very young and even as infants.

Martin Luther and the other Wittenberg reformers were very clear about maintaining the practice of baptizing infants. It was the tradition of Western and Eastern Christianity for well over one thousand years. Holding firm to that tradition with its emphasis on God's action outweighed any notion of having to achieve some appropriate age and cognitive ability. When can you know enough to understand God's grace? When can you do enough to be ready to be taken into God's loving embrace? For Luther and his colleagues, it came down to trusting more in God's action in baptism than in our desire to be baptized. Baptism and its promise as a gift of God's grace and a means to create faith were of far more importance than baptism as a sign of an individual's faith in God. The faith of the church through parents, godparents/ sponsors, pastors, and others first brings a child to those waters and that word of new life. Joined to Christ with the gifts of the Holy Spirit, the child receives faith to grow and trust in God's forgiving grace.

"I am baptized" is an identity that is at once individual and communal. It is "little ol' me" that is individually loved and touched by faith in God's grace. But this me that is baptized is not only united with Christ but also with all those who have been baptized before me and after me. We are one in Christ. We are equal in Christ: equally beloved sisters and brothers of the one who died and was raised again. Christ's history is our history. Christ's future is our future. As soon as I say, "I am baptized," I am proclaiming it with all Christians until the end of time. At the end of the Gospel of Matthew, Jesus' commission to make new disciples by baptizing them in the name of the Father, Son, and Holy Spirit and teaching them to observe all he has commanded is connected with a promise: "and remember, I will be with you always, to the end of the age." Christ is with us in an intimate and mysterious way.

Pastor Scott Moore conducts a baptism in the newly renovated font at Ss. Petri-Pauli (Saints Peter and Paul) Church in Eisleben, Germany. The church where Martin Luther was baptized in 1483 now identifies itself as a Center for Baptism, not only a historical site.

Luther's baptism and ours

Luther thought that the "Old Adam or Eve," our sinful self, should be—and is—drowned in the baptismal waters. Day-old baby Luther was brought to those waters of death and life in Eisleben, Germany, on November 11, 1483, the Feast of St. Martin of Tours. There, with his father and godparents, he was claimed by Christ and named Martin in honor of that saint, a common practice of the day. In anticipation of the observance of the 500th anniversary of the Reformation, the congregation that worships today in that same Eisleben church, Saints Peter and Paul, made a bold move and renovated the worship space to express Luther's theology of baptism more clearly. Next to the remains of the small historic font in which Martin was baptized there is now a prominent baptistery, a font large enough for immersion baptisms. Along the inside rim is an engraving in German of the great commission (Matt. 28:18-20). Luther's baptismal church, more than five hundred years after his own baptism, is now an architectural statement of the baptismal theology he taught.

> Do you not know that all of us who have been baptized into Christ Jesus were baptized into his death? Therefore we have been buried with him by baptism into death, so that, just as Christ was raised from the dead by the glory of the Father, so we too might walk in newness of life. For if we have been united with him in a death like his, we will certainly be united with him in a resurrection like his. [Rom. 6:3-5]

We have been united with Christ in baptism. We can give witness to this mystery and profound theology when we say with Luther and with one another, *baptizatus sum*—I am baptized!

On Holy Communion: The Finite Holds the Infinite

Elizabeth Palmer

Finitum capax infiniti. This Latin phrase means "the finite can hold the infinite." This conviction is at the heart of the way we understand and experience God's grace in the sacrament of holy communion. It also teaches us something about what it means to be bearers of God's grace in a broken world.

Martin Luther found himself engaged in frequent arguments with his theological opponents about the meaning and mechanism of the sacrament of holy communion. How could bread and wine *be* Christ's body and blood? How is it possible that something as expansive as divine grace comes to us through a tiny piece of bread and a small sip of wine? What kind of God would be willing to be present in a form that could be chewed up and digested by human beings? Luther answered each of these questions out of his conviction that finite things are capable of carrying infinity within themselves. *Finitum capax infiniti.* The finite holds the infinite.

Finitum capax infiniti means that the bread and the wine of holy communion really do contain the body and blood of Christ—or as Lutherans often say, Jesus' body and blood are "in, with, and under" the bread and wine. When Jesus said, "This is my body, which is given for you" (Luke 22:19), he wasn't speaking metaphorically or symbolically. The bread and wine don't *remind* us of Christ's body and blood. They don't *represent* body and blood. And they don't *turn into* body and blood. They simply *are* both bread and body, both wine and blood. This doctrine came to be known as "real presence": Christ is really present for us in the bread and wine.

When Luther was challenged to explain philosophically how this can be true, he answered: "What if the philosophers do not grasp it? The Holy Spirit is greater than Aristotle."[1] This is good news for us! It means we don't have to understand rationally a formula that doesn't seem to add up mathematically:

God's Word + bread and wine = body and blood of Christ + forgiveness of sins = infinite grace.

We just trust that it is so, or even just come to the table hoping that it is so. We approach the table yearning for God's mercy to fill us as we taste the morsel of bread and the sip of wine. And it will be so. Because even the smallest bread crumb and the tiniest drop of wine in the sacrament contain the fullness of God's grace. *Finitum capax infiniti.* The finite holds the infinite.

Power made perfect in weakness

One of the less comfortable aspects of holy communion is the idea that we might be eating *God* (or at least eating Jesus Christ, who *is* God). Some of

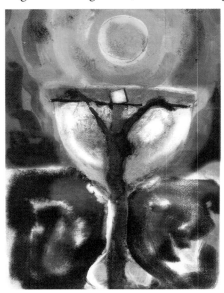

Luther's fiercest opponents argued that the idea of Jesus' body and blood being eaten was disrespectful to the glory of God. Why would a majestic and all-powerful God deign to travel through the digestive system of humans? Luther responded with what we know about God from the Bible. What we know about divine glory is that it suffered death on a cross to bring about the world's salvation. What we know about divine power is that it is made perfect in weakness. What we know about divine majesty is that it was born in a lowly stable.

The Eucharist, by Daniel Bonnell

1. Martin Luther, "The Pagan Servitude of the Church," in *Martin Luther: Selections from His Writings*, ed. John Dillenberger (Garden City, N.Y.: Anchor Books, 1962), 270.

Jesus demonstrates that nothing on this earth is too lowly for God to stoop into. And so we might even think about holy communion the way a poet has:

> There must have been extra wheat flour that day
> for young and old, with and without teeth,
> the virtuous and the ugly
> we all walked away from the altar pursing our lips
> pulling with our blunt tongues at the germ that remained stuck
> between tooth and gum.
>
> Long, slow and swaying lines of penitents
> walking with bovine grace to our seats, nose to tail.
>
> We have eaten God
> and as we stroll to our seats and smile and nod at friends
> we clean Him from our teeth.[2]

Finitum capax infiniti. The finite holds the infinite. God isn't too big or too glorious to inhabit tiny, earthy, imperfect things.

And that's good news for us too. It means that our finite, sinful, human bodies can also be carriers of God's grace and mercy. Every time we receive the sacrament alongside family, pew-mates, and strangers, we are transformed into Christ's living body—an expansion of God's grace into individual bodies who will eventually scatter throughout the neighborhood or city or world to feed the hungry and work for justice. *Finitum capax infiniti.* Despite our finitude, we carry within us the infinite love of God.

Danger or gracious gift?

The intersection of God with earthly elements is beautiful, but it can also feel like a dangerous place to inhabit. We might worry as we approach the communion table that we aren't doing it exactly right; that we don't deserve it; that we aren't invested enough or thinking about it enough. Even Martin Luther had these concerns at times in his life. But eventually he came to realize that holy communion is pure gift. It's not our work; it's God's work through Christ by the power of the Holy Spirit. It's *given* for us.

---

2. "The Feast," by Chuck Huff, in *Simul: Lutheran Voices in Poetry*, ed. Mark Patrick Odland (Maitland, Fla.: Xulon Press, 2007), 31. Reprinted by permission of the poet.

This is good news too: it frees us from worrying about how we think about or practice holy communion. So it doesn't matter what kind of bread or wine we use; whether the bread contains gluten or the wine contains alcohol. It doesn't matter if we understand it rationally or find ourselves puzzled by the mystery of it all. It doesn't matter if we call it eucharist (the Greek word for thanksgiving) or the Lord's supper (which reminds us of Jesus' promises at the last supper) or holy communion (which reminds us that we're part of a much larger group of God's children spanning all of space and time) or the meal (which reminds us that there is holiness, too, in the everyday meals we share with one another outside the church walls). It doesn't matter if we first receive the sacrament as a child or after

> **Despite our finitude, we carry within us the infinite love of God.**

confirmation or later in life. It doesn't matter if we feel something special while receiving communion or if our minds are distracted by our afternoon plans or the funny shoes on the stranger next to us or the baby fussing in the narthex. It doesn't matter if we commune daily or weekly or monthly (although more and more congregations are celebrating communion every Sunday in commemoration of Jesus' resurrection from the dead—and because, after all, the infinite can never run out). It doesn't matter if we can't figure out why we need to be saved, or if we're thinking enough about God's grace.

What matters is that the bread and the wine are Jesus' body and blood, given for us. What matters is that these finite elements contain an infinite measure of God's grace. What matters is that this grace fills us finite creatures until we are overflowing with it—so that we too can go forth and love the neighbor, feed the hungry, advocate for the suffering, and bring healing to our broken world.

Finitum capax infiniti. Thanks be to God!

Luther, Music, and the Reformation

Kathryn A. Kleinhans

AN INTERVIEW WITH SARAH HERZER, KANTORIN OF THE CASTLE CHURCH IN WITTENBERG

What do we know about Martin Luther's abilities as a musician?

First, let me say that Luther loved music! He considered music a gift from God, and therefore we should sing to give thanks to God.

We know that Luther was trained in the church music of his time. As a choir boy at the cathedral school in Magdeburg, Luther would have sung the liturgy of the hours on a daily basis. [The liturgy of the hours consisted of several worship services spread throughout the day, to mark the passage of time with prayer and praise.] Later, as a student at the Latin school in Eisenach, Luther continued to sing in the choir. He was also part of a group of *Kurrende* singers, a traveling choir that went door to door throughout the town in order to earn money to help pay for their schooling. We might think of them as carolers—but not just for Christmas. I know people in Wittenberg who did this on Sunday mornings as recently as the 1950s.

It's also important to know that Luther was well trained in the musical theory of the time. There were two aspects of the study of music in the early sixteenth century: *musica practica* and *musica speculativa. Musica practica*, or "practical music," is music that is heard and performed. *Musica speculativa,* or "speculative music," is the idea that the universe is organized according to mathematical proportions that create a harmony of the universe itself, sometimes referred to as "the music of the spheres." We hear this understanding expressed in Maltbie D. Babcock's familiar nineteenth-century hymn "This is my Father's world, and to my listening ears all nature sings, and round me rings the music of the spheres" (ELW 824). Music theory was a basic component of the liberal arts education Luther (and all students) received at the University of Erfurt.

Vocal music was the center of musicianship and practical music at the time. Both within and outside the church, the focus was on sung music rather than on instrumental performance. Musical instruments were used to support singing or to double the voices. Luther was quite proficient as an instrumentalist on the lute. Yet, strange as this might sound to us, he actually wrote some negative things about the organ, describing it as a loud, overbearing noise.

How was music important for the Reformation?

Developments in Lutheran church music are fairly conservative. Luther and the Lutheran church built upon existing musical traditions. However, liturgical reforms and the wish to incorporate congregational song into worship inspired the creation of a new repertoire of service music made up of hymns and liturgical songs. Also, the celebration of the mass in the vernacular [the language of the people] made it necessary to create church music in German.

Creating church music in the vernacular required a great deal of skill. Thomas Müntzer, another sixteenth-century reformer, whose views were more radical than Luther's, started translating Latin hymns and liturgy into German even before Luther did, but Luther hated Müntzer's translations. They were too literal. When you translate musical texts literally, word for word, you end up with the accented syllables of words falling on unaccented musical notes. The result just isn't good music. Luther's sentiment toward Müntzer was, "How could you kill this music with these words?!"

Luther understood the need to make text and music work together! So he started making his own translations and even writing his own hymns. In fact, there's part of a motet that is attributed to Luther, so we assume he could compose and arrange music in the polyphonic style of the sixteenth century.

Music was the medium that was able to reach the broad masses of people. Luther incorporated music into worship in a way that met people where they were but opened them up to new things. The word liturgy literally means "the work of the people." Luther used music in worship to make Reformation worship something of the people. Church music was no longer something the choir was doing in the choir loft or the priest up in the front of the church. The people sang! And people could buy a hymnal of their own. It's amazing how many hymnals were sold during the early years of the Reformation. Active participation of the broad public helped make the Reformation strong.

It's worth noting that Luther and sixteenth-century Swiss reformer John Calvin had basically the same educational background. Both were versed in the music theory and musical practice of the time. But they went in very different directions. Calvin, I think, was also a choir scholar and must have done the same liturgical singing Luther did as a young student. Like Luther, Calvin knew the power music had to move people, but Calvin was skeptical about how this power could he used; he was concerned that the devil might work through the music to move people in a bad way.

> **"**
> *Luther incorporated music into worship in a way that met people where they were but opened them up to new things.*
> **"**

Luther, however, trusted that music was a gift from God that could be used both to express faith and to evoke faith. In his introduction to the *Bapst Hymnal* in 1545, Luther wrote: "For God hath made our heart and mind joyful through his dear Son whom he hath given for us to redeem us from sin, death and the devil. Who earnestly believes this cannot but sing and speak thereof with joy and delight, that others also may hear and come." Luther identified music as an instrument through which the Holy Spirit works and said that the only thing of higher value than music was the word of God itself.

Say some more about the role of hymns.

Luther's hymns were teaching tools, almost little sermons. A hymn like "Dear Christians, one and all, rejoice" (ELW 594) conveys a clear sense of teaching the people, teaching about salvation through Christ, about grace.

I said earlier that Luther built upon existing musical traditions. Some of his hymns are versions of earlier Latin hymns, expanded or even corrected to reflect Lutheran theology. Some of Luther's hymns, like "A mighty fortress is our God" (ELW 503–505) and "Out of the depths I cry to you" (ELW 600), are paraphrases of psalms. Others are paraphrases of parts of the liturgy.

The very first Lutheran hymnal, published in 1524, had only eight hymns in it, four written by Martin Luther. By way of contrast, our hymnals today

have more than six hundred hymns. These same hymns were sung every week, over and over. People learned the hymns, even the long ones, by singing them again and again. And by learning the hymns they internalized the basic teachings and stories of the faith.

Luther's hymn "A Mighty Fortress" in an early Lutheran hymnal.

When we look back through history, we see that the Lutheran church embraced music from the beginning, culminating with J. S. Bach and his unbelievably rich symbiosis of word and music. That's maybe the central point: for Lutherans, word and music work together. One might even say that music makes the word more effective. I know that, for myself, the Bible verses that I remember are the ones that I've sung.

Tell us about your work here in Wittenberg.

Since 2003, my husband, Thomas, and I have shared the position of director of music ministry at the Castle Church, the church where Luther's Ninety-Five Theses were posted in 1517. We also share a position on the faculty of the Evangelical [Protestant] Seminary in Wittenberg.

We have a very special situation in Wittenberg in that this is the only seminary in Germany that has a full-time church musician on the faculty. Most seminaries have a church musician who comes in and does a week-long block on church music from time to time. We have the opportunity really to emphasize both the study and the practice of music. All students take a chant class. They also take lessons for continued vocal training.

Our students don't question the historical liturgical forms of church music. They understand that congregations here are rooted in tradition. For example, we still regularly sing a Kyrie that was composed in 1524! But our students are also interested in learning and doing new things. It's not an either/or here.

Our holistic approach to music as a way of understanding and experiencing God's word for us is a huge gift in our work at the Castle Church. We have a large number of international guests worshiping here. Regardless of the language they speak, people can be a part of worship through the music. You don't just sit and listen. You come to understand the word by doing it, by singing it.

What's really important to me is the idea that music unites. It really makes me sad when music is used as a reason to divide congregations. Luther was faithful to the traditions of church music while also being open to the new. As we teach our students, it's not an either/or. Our common goal is to unite people in the biblical word through music.

J. S. Bach as Theologian-Musician

Karen Black

While the Lutheran church claims many musicians and compos-
ers throughout history, the one most often cited as the greatest is Johann Sebastian Bach (1685–1750). His many organ
and keyboard works, secular orchestral music, and choral cantatas form a
repertoire often performed in the church and concert hall and most certainly studied by any serious composer yet today. Because of his mastery
of compositional craft and depth of musical expression, Bach is considered
one of, if not *the* greatest composer of all Western musical history. But
Bach was also a practicing church musician concerned with many of the
same tasks as church musicians today: rehearsing choirs and instrumental-
ists, meeting with pastors, planning and practicing music for services every
week of the year. His compositions show a deep theological understanding
and a personal faith; his music was often signed with the phrase *Soli Deo
gloria*, to God alone the glory.

Bach spent the first ten years of life in Eisenach, a central German
Thuringian city well known at the time for its fine music. It was also the city
where Martin Luther had spent three years as a student. The Bach family
even lived on Lutherstrasse (Luther Street). In this city steeped in Lutheranism and music traditions, Bach's father was a town musician whose duties
included directing music at the town hall and playing at St. George's Church
on Sunday. Like Luther before him, Bach attended the Latin school of St.
George's. There he learned the chorales and compositions used in Lutheran

worship, but his training in keyboard, violin, and composition came from elsewhere: his father, his older brother, perhaps other musicians, and his own study. After both of his parents died within a year of each other, Sebastian Bach and his brother Jacob went to Ohrdruf, about twenty-five miles away, to live with their oldest brother Johann Christoph, who was organist at St. Michael's Church.

Education for a cantor

Bach remained in Ohrdruf for five years, from 1695 to 1700. During this time, he attended the *Lyceum Illustre Gleichense*, where he excelled as a student. As in Eisenach, the curriculum centered on religious education: the catechism, Bible, psalms, hymns. The upper classes included studies in science, arithmetic, arts, languages (Latin and Greek), ethics, and biblical theology. After losing financial help, Bach entered St. Michael's School in Lüneberg, a north German town some two hundred miles from Ohrdruf. Bach was the first in his family to progress this far in school. The cantor at the *Lyceum* in Ohrdruf had been a student at St. Michael's in Lüneberg and probably helped Bach get a position as choral scholar there, which gave him the financial means to continue his education. Bach graduated from St. Michael's in 1702.

Although Bach ended his formal schooling at a relatively young age, the reputation of the schools he attended, the rigor and breadth of the curriculum, his class rank and reports of excellence as a student, and the will to continue his studies under difficult personal circumstances invite us to consider Bach as a scholar for his time. Bach was not merely a musician, composer, or cantor, but, as Christoph Wolff subtitles his biography, Bach was indeed *the learned musician.*

Photograph of a portion of Bach's "St. Matthew Passion."

Between 1703 and 1723, Bach held many different positions: court musician in Weimar, organist at the New Church in Arnstadt, organist at St. Blasius in Mühlhausen, organist and later concertmaster in the court of the duke in Weimar, and *Capellmeister* at the court of Prince Leopold at Cöthen. During this time Bach married twice: first to Maria Barbara, who bore him seven children (three of whom died as infants), and, following her death, to Anna Magdelena, with whom he had another thirteen children.

Ministry in Leipzig

In 1723, Bach became the cantor at St. Thomas Church in Leipzig, where he remained until his death in 1750. Here he was responsible for music at four churches in Leipzig as well as teaching students at the Latin school at St. Thomas. Although he had composed cantatas in earlier positions, it was in Leipzig that Bach wrote and prepared a cantata to be performed during worship each Sunday of the year (except in Advent and Lent) and for other festivals. A cantata is a large multimovement choral and instrumental composition meant to serve as musical commentary on the readings and theme for the Sunday, a kind of musical sermon. Texts included the Lutheran chorales known by worshipers of the day, as well as other biblical and poetic texts added to expand on the theme. Among Bach's last works was the massive Mass in B Minor, one of the greatest choral works of all time.

> **Bach was the quintessential Lutheran church musician, living as a servant of the church through his vocation as musician.**

Bach was a practicing, practical church musician. Known today primarily as a composer, the discussion of Bach and theology centers on his faith expressed in musical ways in his compositions. A Bible owned by Bach has an annotation next to a section of 2 Chronicles that describes the presence of God in temple worship; Bach's notation reads "Where there is devotional music, God is always at hand with his gracious presence." Bach's extensive personal library of theological writings indicates that he continued to be interested in theological issues and furthered his understanding through personal study throughout his life.

For nearly all of his career Bach was involved in active service to the church, as organist and cantor for court and city. Composition was certainly an important part of his work, but he was also charged with hiring and rehearsing musicians, planning music for worship, and teaching individual students and choristers. We also know that he possessed great skill as an organist. Bach was the quintessential Lutheran church musician, living as a servant of the church through his vocation as musician. Three hundred years later, his life and music continue to be a meaningful and seemingly unending source of spiritual inspiration for many.

For further reading

Christoph Wolff. *Johann Sebastian Bach: The Learned Musician* (New York: W. W. Norton, 2000).

The Reformation and Art

Wanda Deifelt

Many of Martin Luther's views on visual art were developed through his disagreements with Andreas Bodenstein von Karlstadt, one of his colleagues at the University of Wittenberg. While Luther was in hiding at the Wartburg Castle (1521–1522), Karlstadt had become a leader of the movement in Wittenberg and took upon himself the task to demolish everything connected with the Roman mass, including images and vestments. Iconoclasm—the rejection or destruction of religious images—seemed to be gaining control. The main argument employed by the iconoclasts was the biblical prohibition of worshiping idols: we should worship only God and no images. Luther, hearing about the excesses that the iconoclastic ideas provoked, decided to return to Wittenberg and preach against the destructive mob. In his Eight Sermons at Wittenberg (1522), Luther explained that religious images are not necessary, but that Christians "are free to have them or not," as long as they are not worshiped (LW 51:81).

For Luther, the point was not the image itself, but the message and engagement with God that images enable. Religious images can be useful tools for Christian life as long as the heart does not place its trust in them. The word of God can capture our hearts and enlighten us by way of outward things, such as images. If this is their purpose, there is no harm in them and they can help preach and teach the gospel.

The invention of the printing press and the availability of paper, as well as the proliferation of universities—between 1300 and 1500 the number of European universities grew from twenty to seventy—facilitated the wide circulation of information and ideas, including Martin Luther's writings. However, this was not available for the entire population. It is estimated that less than 5 percent of the population in Europe was literate, and of those not all could understand and interpret the theological ideas the reformers wanted to convey. To reach a wider audience, besides making use of the spoken word (sermons) or the written word (books and pamphlets), music and art were also needed. Thus, pictures were included in Luther's translation of the Bible, for the sake of better understanding.

Art as religious education

In "Against the Heavenly Prophets in the Matter of Images and Sacraments," Luther wrote: "It is to be sure better to paint pictures on walls of how God created the world, how Noah built the ark, and whatever other good stories there may be, than to paint shameless worldly things. Yes, would to God that I could persuade the rich and the mighty that they would permit the whole Bible to be painted on houses, on the inside and outside, so that all can see it. That would be a Christian work" (LW 40:99).

One artist in particular, Lucas Cranach the Elder (1472–1553), was instrumental in disseminating the new ideas of the Reformation. He moved to Wittenberg in 1505, when he was appointed to the court of Frederick III, elector of Saxony, as the court painter. Besides being a painter and printmaker, Cranach owned an apothecary and ran a wine pub. In 1522 he printed the first editions of Luther's German translation of the New Testament. Cranach

> **"**
> *To reach a wider audience, besides making use of the spoken word or the written word, music and art were also needed.*
> **"**

was not only a wealthy businessman but also a member of the Wittenberg city council; he was elected mayor three times. He and his wife, Barbara, had five children. Two of them, Hans and Lucas Cranach, worked with their father in the workshop, producing several thousand paintings, engravings, and prints. The workshop employed as many as fifteen artists.

Cranach became a close friend of Luther. He embraced the cause of the Reformation with enthusiasm and found new ways to convey Luther's religious concerns both in art and publication. One of the theological accomplishments of the Reformation was translating the Bible into the vernacular

Altarpiece in St. Mary's Church, Wittenberg.

language, German. Cranach's workshop not only enabled its printing but also provided the artwork for the illustrations. As the theologians translated words from one language to another, it was up to the artists to translate these ideas to an audience that went beyond the literary world.

Messages from an altarpiece

One of the best examples of how art was able to convey religious meaning to a wider audience is the Wittenberg altarpiece of 1547, at the town church of St. Mary's. This parish church had seen the ordination of Protestant ministers since 1534. They were responsible for preaching the gospel, administering the sacraments, and supporting the parishioners. The community itself wanted to leave a testament of the key teachings of the Reformation and so commissioned Cranach the Elder to do the altar painting.

The *predella*, or bottom panel of the painting, shows Martin Luther preaching Christ crucified. Christ's limp body is embraced by a smoke-like loincloth, wafting in either direction. Cranach's rendition contrasts with other contemporary crucifixes, depicting less blood from Jesus' side (Catholic artists drew multiple wounds and spattered blood). Christ's serene facial expression in the Wittenberg altarpiece also contrasts with the agonized facial features portrayed in Catholic crucifixes of the time. The message is the centrality of the cross and the good news of forgiveness, which Luther preaches from a wall-niche pulpit. While holding steadfast to the scriptures, Luther points toward the central figure of Christ. Katharina von Bora, Luther's wife, and their son are joined by the congregants. Together, they pay close attention to the message of the gospel presented through the cross and the word being preached.

The center panel depicts the eucharist (Lord's supper). The circular table contrasts with other famous paintings of the last supper: there is no head of the table because all are in Christ and are Christ to one another. Cranach models the twelve disciples after actual citizens of Wittenberg. Luther is easily recognized in the painting: he is the one receiving the chalice. This reminds the community that Luther returned the communion cup to the parish. At the start of the sixteenth century only clergy received the blood of Christ by drinking the wine. The laity received only the bread, or body of Christ. Luther challenged this misinterpretation in his treatise "The Babylonian Captivity of the Church." Sitting in front of Luther is Hans Luft, a printer who published the complete German Bible. Maurice of Saxony is depicted as Judas. He had originally supported the Reformation but then betrayed its ideals for his own gain. And yet, Jesus feeds a morsel of bread to Judas, demonstrating that the good news of justification extends to everybody, even the unworthy.

Despite the equality among them, the cup bearer is dressed as a noble, reminding the viewer that "whoever wishes to be great among you must be your servant." The waiter is Lucas Cranach the Younger. This is a paradigm for the role of secular authority and leaders, whose function is to serve, not to be served.

As a reflection of Luther's teaching regarding the real presence of Christ in, with, and under the forms of bread and wine, Cranach's painting shows the presence of Christ in multiple ways: as the food on the table (the sacrificial lamb), as the one who is serving the disciples, and as the community gathered around the table.

The left panel of the altarpiece shows Philipp Melanchthon baptizing an infant. The baptismal font is big enough for a total immersion, which Luther considered a symbol of the sinful self being drowned so that a new person could be raised up. Every day Christians were to renew their baptism, drowning sins and being born anew. It may seem puzzling that Melanchthon is doing the baptism, since he was not an ordained pastor; he was a scholar and theologian. Because of the nature of baptism, however, all Christians become part of the royal priesthood, having not only the chance but also the responsibility to bring others to Christ.

The right panel shows Johannes Bugenhagen, pastor of the parish church, sitting in an open confessional and exercising the office of the keys, a symbol of forgiveness according to Matthew 16:19. The pious man is absolved. He is on his knees and is truly repentant, so the pastor unlocks heaven's doors for him. The other man is arrogant. He has his hands tied, perhaps signifying that he is still in bondage to sin, so the keys are held against his back. Luther initially counted confession among the sacraments, but later insisted that only baptism and eucharist are sacraments, because they are visible signs of grace commanded by Jesus. The scene shown here portrays the "hearing of faith" held by Luther and other reformers on the eve of attending the Lord's supper.

Cranach's contribution to the Reformation, especially to the work of Luther, is undeniable. Through his art, he served as an interpreter of Luther's theology. The Wittenberg altar is a testament to the power of images and their capacity to enable better understanding, to serve as memorial, and to bear witness to the word of God. Sometimes, a picture can be worth more than a thousand words!

Faith Active in Love

Luther's understanding of the gospel as God's gift of grace through faith in Jesus Christ was tremendously freeing! Liberated from focusing on what and how much one needed to do to please God, the Christian was now free to live for others. God does not need our good works, Luther often said, but our neighbors do. In his 1520 masterpiece, *The Freedom of a Christian*, Luther made this bold claim: "As our heavenly Father supported us freely in Christ, so also we ought freely to support our neighbor with our body and its actions, and each person ought to become to the other a kind of Christ, so that we may be Christs to one another and be the same Christ in all, that is, truly Christians!"[1]

This is an expression of Luther's developing understanding of vocation. Instead of thinking of vocation as a strictly religious term for church professionals (as was the case in the church of Luther's day) or as a strictly secular term describing one's job (as became the case later), for Luther vocation referred to God's call to serve the neighbor in all areas of life: home and family, workplace, community, and church. In short, God works in the world through us!

This call to faithful service of others had institutional, as well as individual, consequences for the Reformation and its adherents. Wherever Lutherans have found themselves through the years, they have responded to God's call not only by establishing churches but also by establishing schools and agencies of human care. This work is often named *diakonia*, a Greek word that means both ministry

---

1. Timothy J. Wengert, ed., *The Annotated Luther,* vol. 1 (Minneapolis: Fortress Press, 2015), 525.

and service. The essays in this section of *Together by Grace* explore many of the ways Lutherans have responded to God's call to care for others and to be stewards of God's created world, thus living out St. Paul's encouragement of "faith working through love" (Gal. 5:6).

Luther on Worship and Welfare

Carter Lindberg

This photo taken at the Luther Museum in Wittenberg shows the original Common Chest. It is a heavy iron-clad strongbox with three independent locks that was kept in the town church for welfare funds. The Common Chest symbolizes Luther's contribution to a radical shift from medieval charity as almsgiving to modern social welfare. Medieval charity, rooted in verses from the Apocryphal books of Tobit and Ecclesiasticus, which stated that almsgiving forgives sins, was understood to serve the donor more than the needy. Even better than modern philanthropy, which often gains the donor public acclaim and perhaps even gets his or her name emblazoned on a building, medieval donations purchased paradise. Indeed, the theology of the medieval church held that the poor were necessary to give the rich occasions for charitable good

This "Common Chest," in the Luther House museum in Wittenberg, Germany, was equipped with three separate locks and keys in order to protect the community's welfare funds from theft or misappropriation.

works. Luther shattered this ideology with his recovery of the radical gospel of salvation by grace alone. As he noted in reflecting on Hebrews 9:15-17, we are named in God's last will and testament, and since the testator, God in Christ, has died the will is now in effect. No matter what a wretch you are, if you are named in the will you get the inheritance (LW 35:88). Freed from anxiety about salvation, Luther perceived that faith may now be active not for my egocentric desires (such as getting to heaven) but for service to the neighbor. The proclamation of free grace and its social consequences clearly caught the attention of medieval folks anxious not only about heaven but also about jobs and making ends meet.

Luther's concern for social welfare, including efforts for government regulation of banking and interest rates, was rooted in worship. He understood social activism for systemic change to benefit the poor as "the liturgy after the liturgy," a work of the people flowing from worship. Worship thrusts the Christian into the world to serve the neighbor. Thus, in his 1523 "Preface" to the city of Leisnig's ordinance for community welfare, Luther wrote: "Now there is no greater service of God [*gottis dienst*, i.e., 'worship'] than Christian love which helps and serves the needy, as Christ himself will judge and testify at the Last Day" (LW 45:172). Similarly, Luther understood Christian vocation to be worship in the realm of the world where we are called to serve the neighbor.

Luther and his colleagues were not utopian in this vision of vocation. They were too profoundly impressed by personal and corporate sin to believe in the possibility of a sinless society this side of eternity. Their goal was not moral perfection but the systemic change of social structures. Grace alone liberates the Christian to engage social and political structures for the common good.

Theology in the form of action

Wherever the Reformation took root, legislation was developed that translated Luther's theology into social programs. The model for these developments was the Wittenberg Order passed by the town council with Luther's help in 1520–1521 and further improved in 1522. A Common Chest was established for funds to assist the poor. The legislation included low-interest loans (4 percent) for workers and artisans; subsidized education and training for children; dowries for poor women so they could marry; job training support for both the unemployed and underemployed; supplies of food and firewood for the needy; and support for a town doctor to care for the poor. The only criterion for support was the need of the recipient. Begging, particularly the widespread medieval practice of monks and mendicant friars, was forbidden because religious begging as well as other scams siphoned off needed funds for the truly poor. Luther wanted to move social welfare from the vagaries of personal feelings and egocentric claims for good works to a rational, legal, institutional structure.

The next major welfare ordinance was that of the town of Leisnig, where in 1522 and 1523 Luther helped develop comprehensive legislation providing relief for the poor as well as reform of worship. The organization and principles of the Leisnig Common Chest included the annual election of ten directors, two each from the nobility and the city council and three each from the citizenry and the rural peasantry. Three detailed record books were to be kept in the chest, which was locked with four different locks and kept in a secure place in the church. The keys were assigned to the representative directors, who were to give triennial reports to the whole community. The initial funding came from properties and funds expropriated from the church. Should there not be sufficient funds, it was decreed that citizens pay taxes assessed by the general assembly to support the welfare program.

Freed to serve others

Luther's fundamental theological shift to grace alone liberated people to go beyond individual charity tied to the achievement of good works and enabled persons in community to serve the common good. In brief, social welfare was rationalized and secularized: rationalized in the sense that reason, now freed from otherworldly constraints, could focus on this-world solutions to social problems, and secularized in the sense that government now was freed from church dominance to seek such solutions. Luther had no illusions that this shift would create the great society.

In his preface to the Leisnig Order he expressed concern that princes would try to grab funds for their own use. One role of the preaching office, he argued, was to expose such greed and thus create calls for reforms and improved legislation. Luther was no slouch in reminding political authorities of their responsibilities. He insisted that government is not only responsible for defending its people but also for nurturing and educating them: ". . . to help the poor, the orphans, and the widows to justice and to further their cause" (LW 13:53). In regard to the fourth petition of the Lord's Prayer, Luther noted in the Large Catechism that coats of arms and coins should be emblazoned and stamped with "a loaf of bread instead of a lion . . . to remind both princes and subjects that it is through the princes' office that we enjoy protection and peace and that without them we could neither eat nor preserve the precious gift of bread."[1] A prophetic task of the preacher "in the congregation" is to unmask injustice "openly and boldly before God and men" (LW 13:49–51).

The other issue Luther had to confront was the perennial complaint that redistribution of wealth short shrifts the deserving "us" to the benefit of the undeserving "them." Centuries before the late Brazilian Archbishop Dom Hélder Câmara (1909–1999), Luther experienced a sixteenth-century version of Câmara's famous statement: "When I feed the poor, they call me a saint; when I ask why people are poor, they call me a communist." On the one hand Luther endorsed the literature of the time that exposed welfare scams (LW 59:236–38). On the other hand, to the objection that social welfare was open to abuse, Luther replied: "He who has nothing to live should be aided. If he deceives us, what then? He must be aided again" (LW 30:278).

In a remarkably short time, these reforms of worship and welfare became models for similar efforts throughout the empire and Scandinavia, eventually informing modern developments of national health care systems, public education, and dignified support for the aged, ill, and unemployed.

For further reading

Carter Lindberg. *Beyond Charity: Reformation Initiatives for the Poor.* Minneapolis: Fortress Press, 1993.

Foster R. McCurley, ed. *Social Ministry in the Lutheran Tradition.* Minneapolis: Fortress Press, 2008.

Samuel Torvend. *Luther and the Hungry Poor.* Minneapolis: Fortress Press, 2008.

Paul Wee. "Reclaiming Luther's Forgotten Economic Reforms for Today," *Lutheran Forum* 48:1 (2014), 52–56.

---

1. "Large Catechism," in Kolb and Wengert, eds., *The Book of Concord* (Minneapolis: Fortress Press, 2000), 450.

Lutherans and *Diakonia*

Susan Wilds McArver

When Martin Luther first posted his Ninety-Five Theses in 1517, he had intended to initiate a scholarly debate about contested matters of theology. He had no idea that his attempted theological reforms would eventually lead to profound repercussions in many other areas of life and society. One such area unintentionally affected deeply by the Reformation was the entire understanding of Christian vocation.

In Luther's day, the only persons said to have a "vocation" were the "professionally holy": bishops, priests, monks, and nuns. Luther, however, emphasized a new understanding of Christian vocation that called for all of life to be lived out in service to God and the neighbor through many occupations, ranging from parenting to shoemaking. A tailor, for example, said Luther, should be able to say that the clothes he made enabled him to earn a living, and, through that living, serve the neighbor. He went on: "Where one Christian does not serve the other, God does not abide there; that is also not Christian living."[1]

In the early and middle part of the nineteenth century, this understanding of life lived in service to the neighbor found particular expression in a program of missional outreach known as the deaconess movement. A number of events pushed the church to ask anew, "Who are my neighbors and how should I serve them?"

Between 1789 and 1815, the French Revolution and the Napoleonic Wars, coupled with the dawn of the industrial revolution, led to enormous social

---

1. Martin Luther, "Sermon in the Castle Church at Weimar, 25 October 1522," in *D. Martin Luthers Werke: Kritische Gesamtausgabe*, vol. 10/ III (Weimar, 1905), 382.

displacement across Europe. The countryside emptied as the desperate and poverty stricken fled for a better life in the rapidly expanding cities of Europe and in the new world of North America. The poor packed into crowded tenements amid squalid conditions, and centuries-old patterns of intergenerational life in small, sheltered communities dissolved.

The question emerged: how should the church respond to these fast-changing and challenging needs of the society?

Inner-mission movement

A number of concerned Christians began to call for a renewed emphasis on service to the neighbor as the true mission of the church—an "inner-mission movement," they called it. "Service" in this context came to involve care for both the neighbor's *physical* needs, as well as for his or her *spiritual* needs, and supporters of the inner-mission movement established a multitude of institutions and agencies to address the desperate problems of the nineteenth-century world.

The Rev. Theodor Fliedner, a Lutheran pastor in Kaiserswerth, Germany, and his wife Friederike (and after her death, his second wife, Caroline), were among those answering this vocational call to social service. The Fliedners began their work with a halfway house for women prisoners in 1833, but within a few short years their ministry had expanded tremendously.

The Fliedners began to train young women, whom they called "deaconesses," to minister in many areas of need, and by the mid-nineteenth century their "inner-mission" work had expanded in all directions. These women received training as nurses, teachers, housemothers, and advocates. They established kindergartens, in the belief that one had to reach children by the age of two or three in a Christian setting in order to lay a necessary foundation for life. They founded mental hospitals, in a day when mental illness was often mistreated and almost always misunderstood. In every ministry they undertook, they reached out to the poor, the dispossessed, and the most marginal members of society to address those with the greatest physical and spiritual needs.

Initially, Fliedner encountered opposition to his desire to place women at the forefront of such work. Into the mid-nineteenth century, for example, nursing was considered extremely inappropriate for respectable women because of the personal and intimate nature of the work. Fliedner, however, persevered, and he proved crucial in the establishment of nursing as a respected profession, especially through the efforts of his most famous student, Florence Nightingale. Although never a deaconess herself, Nightingale received her initial training as a nurse from the institution at Kaiserswerth, and she later wrote a book introducing the ministry of the Fliedners to an English-speaking world.

Training for deaconesses followed a pattern that included life in a motherhouse and the wearing of a distinctive garb. Deaconesses were called "sisters," although unlike Catholic sisters they signed up for a five-year renewable term of service, rather than making a lifelong vow. The Fliedners combined preparation for nursing, teaching, and other skills with intentional times for daily chapel, meditation, Bible reading, and prayer. The deaconess communities learned early on that such a focus on one's inner spiritual life was necessary, because the work of service demanded so much. Deaconesses drew on worship, Bible study, and what we would today call "spiritual formation" to strengthen them for the inevitable challenges of their daily ministry.

The obvious needs of the world and the work of the deaconesses in Germany soon spread the influence of Kaiserswerth across denominations and around the world.

Passavant and American deaconesses

By 1849, the Rev. William Passavant of Pennsylvania had brought deaconesses to North America, and deaconess motherhouses in both Philadelphia and Baltimore were established by 1888 and 1895, respectively. As each ethnic group of Lutherans established themselves more firmly in the new world, they also founded their own deaconess communities. Norwegian Lutherans instituted communities in Brooklyn, Minneapolis, and Chicago. The Swedes started their deaconess communities in Omaha and Minnesota, and the Danes established ministries in the Danish West Indies (now the U.S. Virgin Islands) and Brush, Colorado.

Deaconesses worked in orphanages, prisons, schools, hospitals, hospices, and institutions for children and adults with mental or physical challenges. In each case, women found important, meaningful work through ministry to and service with the neighbor through the church, at a time when few such opportunities for women existed. Through their example, deaconesses exemplified Jesus' ministry of mercy to the most wretched of society, those most often left behind in the rush to the modern world.

Today the legacy of the deaconess and inner-mission movement finds expression in at least two important ways. First, many our most important and well-known Lutheran social service agencies can trace their origins directly to the work of these deaconesses and other pioneers of inner-missions. Many of the orphanages, "industrial schools," and other ministries of the nineteenth century survive and thrive today as group homes for those with special needs, adult care facilities, major medical centers, and as organizations within Lutheran Services in America.

An additional legacy continues through two ministry rosters of the ELCA—the Deaconess Community of the ELCA and the ELCIC (Evangelical Lutheran Church in Canada), and in the newer roster of diaconal ministers, formed in 1993, which includes both men and women called to do the work of the servant on behalf of Christ.

In ways similar to their nineteenth- and early twentieth-century predecessors, today's deaconesses and diaconal ministers serve as bridges between church and world—bringing the ministry of the church to bear on the needs of the world, and bringing the needs of the world back to the mindfulness of the church. They work in ways as diverse as their earlier counterparts did—as chaplains, hospice workers, workers with children and adults, counselors, musicians, teachers, and, yes, as nurses.

> **"**
> *Today's deaconesses and diaconal ministers serve as bridges between church and world.*
> **"**

Sister Elizabeth Fedde, a Norwegian deaconess who worked tirelessly to establish a hospital in Brooklyn that ministered to some of the poorest immigrants landing on North American shores in the late nineteenth century, sometimes felt discouraged by the great needs she witnessed, contrasted with the small contribution she felt she as an individual could make. But she also knew that she represented something larger than herself in her work. As she told her fellow deaconesses, "You sisters are the Bible your patients will read." Today, the Lutheran Medical Center and Lutheran Health Care in New York continue her groundbreaking work, still addressing the needs of those who are often the most forgotten in our contemporary world, ministering in languages ranging from Hebrew and Chinese to Arabic.

Across our society, deaconesses and diaconal ministers remain living witnesses to the gospel call to love the neighbor. To rephrase Luther's quotation slightly, "When a Christian serves the other, God is present; that is Christian living." Building on the past, today's deaconesses and diaconal ministers live out this reality daily in all that they do.

Making Malaria History

Jessica Nipp Hacker

I thank my God every time I remember you, constantly praying with joy in every one of my prayers for all of you, because of your sharing in the gospel from the first day until now. I am confident of this, that the one who began a good work among you will bring it to completion by the day of Jesus Christ. (Philippians 1:3-6)

God has indeed begun a good work among us. Malaria has long been a thief of lives and livelihoods. Now it's poised to become history through the efforts of millions across the globe—and Lutherans are a part of the story!

For several years, Lutherans in the United States have turned our hearts and our hands to the realities of this parasite-borne disease, preventable and treatable but still rampant, especially in Africa. Working alongside our sisters and brothers in Africa, American Lutherans have taken concrete steps to put an end to malaria. The ELCA Malaria Campaign and the Lutheran Malaria Initiative offered God's children in the United States the opportunity to walk together with God's children in Africa as they work to uplift communities and infuse lives with health and hope.

> **Working alongside our sisters and brothers in Africa, American Lutherans have taken concrete steps to put an end to malaria.**

Seemingly overnight, a transformation occurred in Lutheran congregations all across the United States: infestations of paper mosquitoes popped

up in narthexes and fellowship halls; handy Lutherans erected mosquito nets on frames; thermometers registered "feverish" fundraising progress; Sunday school students began to speak knowledgably about nets, malaria medication, and compassion for all of God's children. Volunteer leaders began to energize their own and neighboring congregations. A movement began, at first a ripple, then a tidal wave of generosity.

Malaria loses ground

Across the world in Africa, similar transformation was brewing. Lutheran churches and social service organizations, undergirded by support from brothers and sisters in the United States, sought expert staff and began training a network of volunteers. Lutheran programs supplied local clinics and volunteer leaders with rapid diagnostic tests, first-line malaria medications, and enough mosquito nets to go around. Communities began to come together to learn the signs and symptoms of malaria, behaviors to keep their families safe from mosquitoes, and how to hang and mend a mosquito net. Children learned in school and taught their parents; parents learned in community

As of December 31, 2015, programs supported by the ELCA Malaria Campaign:
- **took place in 14 countries**
- **distributed 60,000 insecticide-treated nets**
- **empowered 14,000 households economically**
- **tested 200,000 people, and provided treatment for those who tested positive for malaria**
- **trained 12,000 community members in malaria prevention and treatment**
- **provided 32,000 pregnant women with malaria prevention medication**
- **educated more than 2.3 million people about malaria**

workshops and taught their children. Open clinics brought testing and treatment to the people, eliminating the burden of travel. Lively song, dance, and drama taught memorable, life-saving lessons.

The results piled up: millions of dollars raised, millions of lives touched. In Uganda, Stella is a volunteer trained by the Lutheran program to educate her neighbors about malaria. Stella teaches mosquito control techniques and good hygiene, helps families maintain and use their mosquito nets, connects pregnant women with good prenatal care, and intervenes immediately when someone falls ill with malaria. She works hard to make her dream of a malaria-free future come true for her community.

"I speak with pride," Stella says. "Now people know how to fight the enemy: the anopheles mosquito. The majority of people in my community are now using nets and getting treatment. If you go to the five sub-counties where the [Lutheran] program is at work, you see the impact."

The statistics agree. When the program in Uganda began, 92 percent of households had experienced a case of malaria in the past month. Thanks to Stella and her colleagues, that number is down to just 45 percent. And 98 percent of households in the program area now have at least one insecticide-treated mosquito net.

Oceans apart but connected by love of Christ and love of neighbor, Lutherans are changing lives. We are lifting prayers of joy because of our sharing in the gospel—and we trust that the one who began this work among us will bring it to completion!

Organizing to Serve

Kathryn A. Kleinhans

LUTHERAN IMMIGRATION AND REFUGEE SERVICE, LUTHERAN WORLD RELIEF, AND LUTHERAN SERVICES IN AMERICA

Lutheran Immigration and Refugee Service

The work of Lutherans in resettling refugees gained public attention with the release of Clint Eastwood's 2008 movie *Gran Torino*. Eastwood plays Walt Kowalski, an embittered Korean War veteran who over time develops a relationship with the Hmong family living next door. In one scene Walt asks how and why the Hmong came to the Midwest. His neighbor Sue answers, "Blame the Lutherans. They brought us over." Walt responds, "Everybody blames the Lutherans."

In the aftermath of World War I, U.S. Lutherans made efforts to support European refugees. As World War II began in Europe, the number of refugees grew, and in 1939 the organization today known as Lutheran Immigration and Refugee Service (LIRS) was founded. One-third of the displaced persons in Europe after World War II were Lutheran, and it was natural for U.S. Lutherans, the vast majority of whom had immigrant roots themselves, to reach out with a welcoming, helping hand.

Lutheran Immigration and Refugee Service

The Vision and Mission of LIRS

Vision
All migrants and refugees are protected, embraced, and empowered in a world of just and welcoming communities.

Mission
Witnessing to God's love for all people, we stand with and advocate for migrants and refugees, transforming communities through ministries of service and justice.

Since its founding, LIRS has resettled more than 379,000 refugees from around the world, refugees from many countries and of many faiths. This ministry is complex. According to the LIRS website:

Refugees are resettled through a network of 28 local organizations in 26 states, most of which are Lutheran social ministry organizations. Sixteen of those organizations also provide immigration legal services. Asylum seekers, survivors of torture and other migrants impacted by detention are served through 23 partners providing legal and social services including visitation ministry. In addition, we work directly with eight foster care programs at the state level to provide family reunification and foster care services for unaccompanied refugee and immigrant minors.

LIRS is supported by the Evangelical Lutheran Church in America (ELCA), the Lutheran Church—Missouri Synod (LCMS), and the Latvian Evangelical Lutheran Church in America. To learn more, visit www.lirs.org.

Lutheran World Relief

Has your congregation or your women's group ever assembled layettes (baby-care kits), school kits, or quilts to send overseas? If so, you've likely been a part of the ministry of Lutheran World Relief. LWR was founded in 1945 to provide relief to those whose lives and livelihoods were devastated by World War II. Since then,  the ministry of LWR has expanded to include development work as well as the provision of material goods and supplies.

Wars, famine, and natural disasters create emergency situations to which LWR responds swiftly, just as it did in the aftermath of World War II. Poverty, however, is a chronic condition and requires a longer-term strategy. To alleviate poverty and human suffering, LWR works with trusted local partners in many countries to develop sustainable projects in the areas of agriculture, health, education, and more. LWR works from a philosophy of *accompaniment*, "recognizing that communities—no matter how poor—already have resources and assets that can be harnessed for their wellbeing.

> *LWR works from a philosophy of accompaniment, 'recognizing that communities—no matter how poor—already have resources and assets that can be harnessed for their wellbeing.'*

Building on these assets, LWR establishes a relationship with local partners based on mutual trust and respect to create a flexible plan to improve the wellbeing of the poor."

The numbers are impressive:

- In 2015, LWR sent $12.9 million worth of quilts and kits to at least 674,057 people in nineteen countries.
- In 2014, LWR funded 153 development projects reaching 4,763,599 people in thirty-five countries.

Survey results show that U.S. Lutherans see LWR "as a reliable and efficient way to put their Christian faith into action [and] to express their Christian love for neighbors."

"Then the king will say to those at his right hand, 'Come, you that are blessed by my Father, inherit the kingdom prepared for you from the foundation of the world; for I was hungry and you gave me food, I was thirsty and you gave me something to drink, I was a stranger and you welcomed me, I was naked and you gave me clothing, I was sick and you took care of me, I was in prison and you visited me.' Then the righteous will answer him, 'Lord, when was it that we saw you hungry and gave you food, or thirsty and gave you something to drink? And when was it that we saw you a stranger and welcomed you, or naked and gave you clothing? And when was it that we saw you sick or in prison and visited you?' And the king will answer them, 'Truly I tell you, just as you did it to one of the least of these who are members of my family, you did it to me.'" (Matt. 25:34-40)

LWR is supported by the Evangelical Lutheran Church in America (ELCA) and the Lutheran Church—Missouri Synod (LCMS). To learn more, visit www.lwr.org.

Lutheran Services in America

You've doubtless heard the saying, "The whole is greater than the sum of its parts." Perhaps nowhere is this truer than with the work of Lutheran social ministry organizations.

Lutheran Services in America (LSA) was founded in 1997 but has a history stretching back well over 150 years. Its membership, by definition, consists of all social ministry organizations affiliated with the Evangelical Lutheran Church in America (ELCA) or recognized by the Lutheran Church—Missouri Synod (LCMS). This means that more than three hundred health and human services organizations are part of LSA. Together those organizations serve six million people annually. That's a cumulative impact of almost one of every fifty people in the United States!

Different member organizations of LSA provide a range of social services, including senior services, health care, services to children and families, disability services, economic empowerment, and housing and community development. While founded and supported by Lutherans, these social ministry organizations serve anyone in need, regardless of age, race, culture, or religious affiliation. By networking together, member organizations are able to share their expertise, provide enhanced opportunities for leadership development, and advocate for the common good.

You may never hear the name or see a sign for "Lutheran Services in America," but you may well be familiar with one or more or those three-hundred-plus member organizations. From Lutheran Social Services of Alaska to Mision Esperanza in Miami, Florida; from Lutheran HealthCare in Brooklyn, New York, to Bethel New Life in Chicago, to the Navajo Evangelical Lutheran Mission in Arizona; LSA spans the country with a network of care.

To learn more, visit http://www.lutheranservices.org.

The Lutheran Commitment to Education

Stanley N. Olson

Martin Luther was a university professor in Wittenberg, Germany. His Ninety-Five Theses were a public invitation to scholarly debate. The Lutheran reforming movement was fostered in a university atmosphere of careful study and lively discussion. Luther himself quickly became an advocate of education for daily living—for all ages, women and men, girls and boys. Lutherans have sustained and expanded this broad engagement across 500 years because their commitment to education grows directly from the conviction that God calls all people to serve their neighbors. Teaching and learning are still key to discerning our way into God's good future.

Education in the content and practices of Christian faith is essential. Lutheran homes and congregations have a long-standing focus on the faith education of children and youth. Adult learning happens in conversation, in worship, in service contexts, and in a variety of formal and informal education efforts. We know that faith is nourished by continual attention to the Bible, by information and wisdom passed down to us, and by conversation with others who also encounter Christ and those who do not. Seminaries extend this learning in depth and breadth.

Lutheran learning doesn't stop with religious matters. All knowledge and learning is within the concern of God. Thus wherever Lutherans have gone in the world, they have established schools for children and youth, teaching religion and other subjects because they deem all aspects of God's world worthy of study. Around the globe thousands of Lutheran early childhood, primary, and secondary schools serve congregations and communities.

Higher education has been a powerful part of the Lutheran commitment to broad education. In the United States and Canada that commitment led to the establishment and continuing support of excellent colleges and universities that affirm and explore the equal value and the inseparability of what some call the sacred and the secular. To this day, Lutheran higher education sends wise, broadly educated women and men into the world with a commitment to service and to continued learning. These colleges and universities exemplify the Lutheran affirmation of the worth and connectedness of all areas of learning.

Lutherans expect strong education

That sense of worth and connectedness is also seen in the thousands of Lutherans who are teachers and aides, school administrators, and board members at all levels of public education. It is seen in familiar ministries of the church. Lutherans are known for expecting and offering broad and excellent education for their clergy and other church leaders. We expect our servant leaders to help people see connections. Public worship includes sermons, hymns, and prayers that connect us to the world. Youth programs, including outdoor ministries, teach about the Bible, faith, the natural world, leadership, community, and global connections. Campus ministries consider and share faith in the context of the broad learning that happens in public colleges and universities. Hospital, social service agency, military, and corrections chaplains do the same in their contexts. The ELCA and other Lutheran entities foster the study of social concerns and issue statements for learning and guidance. Publishing ministries like Augsburg Fortress enhance the education commitment across a broad range of topics and expand its reach through innovation.

Less visibly but consistently over the centuries Lutherans have been advocates for high-quality public education, available to all. The ELCA reaffirmed this in 2007 with the adoption of a social statement titled "Our Calling in Education," describing a twofold commitment to educate in Christian faith for vocation and to help ensure that all have access to high-quality education for the common good.

The essential connectedness of faith and education can be summarized in a little catechism:

Faith Active in Love

Because of Jesus Christ, the world
Because of the world, vocation
Because of vocation, education
Because of vocation and education, Jesus Christ

Because of Jesus Christ, the world. Christian faith is world affirming because God is world affirming. We confess the ongoing creative work of God. We celebrate the gracious saving action of God in Jesus Christ, sustained by God's Spirit, for the world. In the death and resurrection of Jesus, God engages us with the world, freeing us from self-centeredness—opening our eyes, hearts, and minds to see reality and need.

This engagement with the world is not simple or smooth. Creation is complex and ongoing. At the center of the Jesus story are his suffering and death. It is clear throughout the New Testament that Jesus' followers often find their godly work in the midst of challenge and pain. A Christ-centered view of the world sees the power of sin, the impacts of evil—and sees the powerful potential of joining in God's work right here, in the world.

Because of the world, vocation. By opening us to the world's needs, Christ calls us and shows us how we can serve. This understanding of calling, or vocation, is central for Lutherans. We serve Christ by serving people.

Lutherans use *vocation* as a general description of life in Christ—in baptism we are *called* to serve our neighbors near and far. We also use the term to describe specific callings from God. Christians choose a lifework with the sense that it can be their place to serve specific needs and the common good. That is a vocation. Lutherans also use vocation to describe the multiple roles of life, chosen or not. We have callings as family members, citizens, friends, workers, congregation members, students, and more. Those life roles can be difficult—coping with illness, limitations, special needs—but there is joy and strength in knowing that these callings too are from Christ. And there is hope in knowing that we can support others and be supported in our callings to serve.

Vocation is ministry (service) in daily life. Martin Luther restored the church's insight that all Christians have vocations. In his day, the church taught that only monks, priests, and nuns had vocations. Their work was on a higher level than all other work. Luther didn't demean those church roles, but he insisted that other daily roles were equally pleasing to God—parent, farmer, business, government. Lutherans must still hold this conviction. We are all equally called by Christ to service.

Because of vocation, education. Vocation drives the Lutheran commitment to education because responding to the world's needs requires knowledge and skills. Our callings require education in the Christian faith and about the world that needs our service.

For example, consider the general and specific education needed to respond well as a Christian to the calling as parent, nurse, farmer, mechanic, business leader, teacher, software designer, or government officeholder. There are learning needs even in a relatively simple calling such as helping a neighbor with a household repair or voting in an election.

We seek education to be able to respond well in the vocations we choose and the vocations we discover in our life roles. We need broad, foundational learning, and throughout life we continue to learn specific things, as needed. Vocation drives a personal commitment to education.

> **Our callings require education in the Christian faith and about the world that needs our service.**

Lutherans follow Luther's example in advocating for education for all. In a 1524 address, "To the Councilmen of All Cities in Germany," Luther urged that schools be established for boys and girls so that they could be equipped to respond to the needs around them. Our world is much different from that of the sixteenth century, but this principle holds. All of us have multiple callings, and it is our shared responsibility to foster high quality education for all to help assure that all are able to respond well to their callings.

Because of vocation and education, Jesus Christ. Lutherans work in close partnership with other Christians and with non-Christians to understand and respond to the world's needs and to provide needed education. For us, this reflection and action lead back to the central work of God in Christ. Our learning about the world can deepen our understanding of God, Christ, and the Spirit. Our failures in commitment to service and education should drive us back to our gracious, forgiving God for renewal and inspiration. Lutherans remain convinced that the wisdom of *faith* is inseparably linked with *knowledge* of this wonderful, difficult, complex world and that both lead us to faithful innovation.

Of course, the Lutheran commitment to education has not always been consistent in concept or effective in practice over these centuries. Nor do Lutherans always agree on how to carry out a vocation or how to sustain the needed education. But the calling is clear and persistent: for the sake of serving the world, Lutherans will continue to value education in Christian faith and to value education about the world we serve.

A Lutheran Educator Reflects on Religion and Science

Walter C. Bouzard

In a world before Copernicus and Galileo, conflict between religious and scientific worldviews was generally unknown. It was assumed that the biblical accounts of the cosmos accurately represented the reality of a geocentric (earth-centered) universe. Copernicus hammered a crack in that worldview; Galileo's observations eventually split it apart.

The huge challenge these early scientists posed to the Bible's portrayal of space was compounded by the observations of Charles Darwin and the implications of his work for the history of the world. Darwin's *Origin of the Species* (1859) was almost immediately recognized as a challenge to the widespread assumption that the present world is pretty much the same as the one represented at the end of the first chapter of Genesis, a world then (and in some quarters, still!) thought to have been created in the year 4004 BCE. To the contrary, Darwin marshaled evidence that all species of creatures, including humans, evolved over a huge length of time. Darwin's work raised other troubling questions for many Christians. If Darwin was correct, what were the implications for the truth of the Bible? In what way can human beings be said to have been created in the image of God? And what might all of this say about the nature of a creator God?

Beyond these specific religious questions, scientific inquiries into space and time more generally left open the nature of the relationship between religion and science. Up until the relatively recent past, events for which there were no scientific explanations—diseases and weather, to name but two examples—were relegated to the mysterious will and purposes of God. However, as all branches of science "closed the gaps" in areas that had been consigned to the mysterious operations of God, the need for God's activity as an explanation came into question, as did the role of religion itself.

Four models

Ian Barbour's influential book *Religion in an Age of Science* (1990) still provides the most widely recognized taxonomy for the relationship of religion and science.[1] Barbour describes four models for relating science and religion. The first is the *conflict* model. It pits scientific materialism against biblical literalism. In this model, neither side finds grounds for compromise; religion and science are considered irreconcilable, and individuals must choose one or the other.

Barbour's second way of relating religion and science is the *independence* model. It views science and religion as occupying independent spheres of knowledge and discourse. The two enterprises speak different languages and address different areas of human inquiry; science and religion both make valid truth claims within their respective realms. Independence describes the position fostered by Galileo when he famously quoted Cardinal Baronius, "The Bible was written to show us how to go to heaven, not how the heavens go."[2] More recently, Stephen J. Gould articulated a version of the independence solution. Religion and science, he wrote, represent nonoverlapping *magisteria* ("NOMA"): the sciences treat the material world while religion involves itself with questions of ultimate meaning. The separate realms should refrain from commenting on or making judgments about questions falling under the other's magisterial authority.[3]

A third model for relating religion and science is *dialogue*. It holds that religion and science can be in conversation with each other about those

---

1. Ian G. Barbour's *Religion in an Age of Science* (San Francisco: Harper & Row, 1990) was subsequently expanded and republished as *Religion and Science: Historical and Contemporary Issues* (San Francisco: HarperSanFrancisco, 1997). For the following see the latter volume, pages 77–105.

2. Galileo Galilei, *Discoveries and Opinions of Galileo*, trans. Stillman Drake (Garden City, N.Y.: Doubleday, 1957), 186.

3. Stephen Jay Gould, *Rocks of Ages: Science and Religion in the Fullness of Life* (New York: Ballantine, 1999), 5.

questions that fall outside the methods of science. One point of intersection occurs where science observes that much of the universe is orderly and religion asserts that such order is contingent upon the will and purposes of God. With respect to the creation, for example, the theological assertion that God chose the initial conditions and laws of the universe does not violate scientific laws or explanations. Dialogue over such matters may arise from the experience of awe shared by many scientists and people of faith (although these are not mutually exclusive categories). Ursula Goodenough's *The Sacred Depths of Nature* represents this mode of relating science and religion.[4]

Barbour's fourth model is *integration,* the idea that some measure of blending of the content of theology and the content of science is possible. This may take the form of *natural theology,* a claim that the existence of God can be inferred from the presence of design in nature. This notion is close to the argument of those who, in recent decades, have self-identified as Creationists and, more recently, as Intelligent Design theorists. Beyond this, integration may be articulated as a *theology of nature,* the position that scientific theories and discoveries may lead to the reformulation of theological doctrines. Finally, integration may entail a systematic synthesis of both science and religion, resulting in an inclusive metaphysics such as process theology.

> **There is no inherent conflict between scientific findings and the understanding of God as creator, redeemer and sanctifier.**

North American Lutherans exhibit no homogeneity in their judgments about religion and science. For example, the Lutheran Church—Missouri Synod (LCMS) explicitly rejects Gould's NOMA model on grounds that it "is incompatible with a comprehensive biblical worldview, according to which Christianity is a framework of 'total truth' about reality."[5] The LCMS aligns itself with the *conflict* model. Scripture is *a priori* the sole fount of infallible, inerrant, and divinely inspired truth and thus always subordinates

4. Ursula Goodenough, *The Sacred Depths of Nature* (New York: Oxford University Press, 1998).

5. *In Christ All Things Hold Together: The Intersection of Science & Christian Theology: A Report of the Commission on Theology and Church Relations* (St. Louis: Lutheran Church—Missouri Synod, 2015), 7.

science. Scientific evidence in conflict with scripture is dismissed on grounds of "the fallible nature of science."[6]

The position of the Evangelical Lutheran Church in America (ELCA) approximates Barbour's *independence* model. On the one hand, the ELCA accepts the scriptures "as the inspired Word of God and the authoritative source and norm of its proclamation, faith, and life."[7] Nevertheless, the scriptures reflect the culture in which they were composed. For example, science long ago disproved the flat-earth cosmology of Genesis. Even so, "The sciences, by definition, do not constitute understandings (or imply judgments) about God. There is no inherent conflict between scientific findings and the understanding of God as creator, redeemer and sanctifier."[8]

Science and religion both make valid truth claims within their respective realms. The intersection is the summons for faithful people to use science to care for human communities and God's creation.

---

6. "In Christ All Things Hold Together," 24.

7. ELCA Constitution, 2.03.

8. *A Social Statement on Genetics, Faith and Responsibility* (Chicago: Office of the Presiding Bishop, ELCA, 2011), 4.

Why Lutherans Care for Creation: A Profile

Lutherans Restoring Creation
www.lutheransrestoringcreation.org

Theology. Rooted in the scriptures as received by the theology of Martin Luther and the Lutheran confessional tradition, we affirm God as creator of all, with an incarnation theology that cherishes the continuing presence of God in, with, and under the whole creation. We see redemption through Christ as a "new creation." We experience the Holy Spirit as sustainer of all, straining toward the fulfillment of creation.

Cross and resurrection. The gospel of the cross leads us to see God in solidarity with the human situation and all creation in its pain and agony, especially the most vulnerable humans and other forms of life. A theology of the cross gives us communion with "creation groaning in travail" and stresses that God redeems *all* creation. Justified by grace alone, we are freed to acknowledge our complicity in personal and systemic sin against creation, to repent, and to empty ourselves in service to the Earth community. Our affirmation of resurrection offers hope not only for the world to come but here and now in this world.

Worship and sacraments. We affirm that the material world is good and capable of bearing the divine and that Christ is present in such ordinary elements as grapes, grain, and water—the basis for our delight in and reverence for all creation. Our worship invites us into transforming encounters with

God in the flesh and in the whole natural world. We are called to worship God *with* creation, joining in the song of the whole creation.

Vocation. Our biblical vocation is "to serve and to preserve" Earth. Because the church exists for the sake of the world, we are called to "ongoing reformation" from generation to generation in response to new needs and current crises of this life. Our vocation to economic and ecological justice is an expression of "the care and redemption of all that God has made."

Ethics. We have an ethic of faith-active-in-love for vulnerable neighbors, including the vulnerable throughout the whole Earth community. Liberated from a legalism that limits and enslaves, we live in the freedom to address new situations, such as the ecological state of the world. We do so not to dominate but as servants to the Earth community. We do so not out of fear or guilt or arrogance but joyfully out of gratitude, grace, and love.

> **"**
> *Our affirmation of resurrection offers hope not only for the world to come but here and now in this world.*
> **"**

Social ministry. With a heritage rooted in the Reformation, Lutherans have a history of social service to the poor, the elderly, the sick, the oppressed, the marginalized—through hospitals, homes for the elderly, social ministry agencies, Lutheran Immigration and Refugee Services, Lutheran Disaster Relief, the Malaria Campaign, and Lutheran World Relief. The ELCA's commitment to racial justice and economic justice recognizes that ecological degradation disproportionally devastates communities of color and the poor, both in the United States and globally. We frame all these commitments as the healing and restoring of the Earth community (www.elca.org/careforcreation).

Public witness and advocacy. The ELCA has official social statements on "Caring for Creation" and "Sustainable Livelihood for All," a full-time director of environmental education and advocacy in Washington, D.C., and Lutheran Public Policy offices (www.elca.org/advocacy). The ELCA calls its people "to speak on behalf of this earth, its environment and natural resources and its inhabitants." The ELCA expects its ordained ministers to "be exemplary stewards of the Earth's resources" and to "lead this church in the stewardship of God's creation" (from "Vision and Expectations").

Scholarship and education. Lutheran scholars have taken the lead in promoting ecological theology, ethics, Bible study, and social commentary. ELCA colleges and seminaries have ecological justice programs and Earth-friendly campus lifestyles that prepare Lutherans for leadership in the church and in the world. Continuing education events for clergy and laity highlight creation care.

Caring for creation across the church. Some synods identify themselves as creation-care synods. Synodical and churchwide resolutions call us to address environmental issues. Many Lutheran congregations incorporate Earth-care commitments into their worship, education, property, discipleship at home and work, and public witness. Lutheran outdoor ministries have brought environmental concerns and positive experiences with nature to many youth. The ELCA churchwide office models environmental concerns. The ELCA offers grants for environmental projects. Lutheran theologians have been leaders for more than half a century in proposing a "theology for Earth."

Organizations for earthkeeping. Lutherans have led in the Green Congregation Program, made available care for creation worship (www.letall creationpraise.org), and provided resources and programs through Lutherans Restoring Creation (www.lutheransrestoringcreation.org).

Collaboration. Lutherans continually learn from and applaud the ecological commitments of other religious and ethnic traditions. We are eager to collaborate with other denominations, religions, and secular organizations in addressing the environmental issues of our time, along with the related issues of race, gender inequality, exploitation of the poor, and inequality of wealth.

Lutherans are called to listen to the cry of the Earth along with the cry of the poor and to take leadership in these critical issues. Ecological justice is not an add-on. It is foundational for our faith. This is how we seek to love God in, with, and under all creation: as neighbors of all living things on Earth and as pilgrims with all things in the cosmos. We call upon all persons of good will to be participants, with us, in this, the great work of our time.

The Neighborliness (*Diakonia*) of All Believers

Craig L. Nessan

TOWARD REIMAGINING THE UNIVERSAL PRIESTHOOD

In *The Freedom of a Christian,* Martin Luther asserted that all Christian believers share in the priesthood of Christ. Unfortunately, the practice of the churches that stem from the Reformation has never adequately delivered on the power of this theological claim. In large part, this is because of the continued usage of the term *priesthood* to describe the vocation of the baptized. The metaphor of priesthood perpetuates a clerical misunderstanding of Christian vocation in the world, the notion that real ministry is only what "priests" (clergy) do. The following fifteen theses reimagine and outline an alternative theology for the ministry of the baptized in the world under the concept "the neighborliness (*diakonia*) of all believers."

1. By the power of the gospel of Jesus Christ, God sets Christian people free *from* all that holds them captive to the powers of this world—sin, death, and the power of the devil—freeing them *for* service of the neighbor in this world.
2. In baptism every Christian person has put on the death and resurrection of Jesus Christ. In baptism the Holy Spirit "ordains" every baptized person into the vocation of service to God and neighbor.

3. At the rite of affirmation of baptism, one is asked: "Do you intend to continue in the covenant God made with you in holy baptism: to live among God's faithful people, to hear the word of God and share in the Lord's supper, to proclaim the good news of God in Christ through word and deed, to serve all people, following the example of Jesus, and to strive for justice and peace in all the earth?" To which each Christian person responds: "I do, and I ask God to help and guide me."

4. God's purposes for this world, in contest with the forces of evil, are carried out through two distinctive yet complementary strategies: the right-hand/spiritual strategy of proclaiming the gospel of Jesus Christ to all the world and the left-hand/worldly strategy of providing structure and order to the created world. God employs the baptized in both of these strategies as *the primary agents* to accomplish God's purpose of bringing life to the world.

> **In baptism the Holy Spirit 'ordains' every baptized person into the vocation of service to God and neighbor.**

5. "To equip the saints for the work of ministry, for building up the body of Christ" (Eph. 4:12) encompasses formation and education both for the right-hand strategy of speaking the gospel to others (the ministry of evangelizing) and for the left-hand strategy of service to others through four distinct arenas of life which God has instituted in the created world (the ministry of shalom).

6. Evangelizing begins with the art of evangelical listening to others and taking seriously the concrete situation of those with whom we speak; then, drawing authentically from one's own experience, evangelizing involves speaking the promises of the faith, explicitly naming the reality of God's work in Christ by the power of the Holy Spirit.

7. Shalom ministry—which encompasses peacemaking, social justice, care for creation, and respect for inherent human dignity—is lived out as Christian neighborliness in the four primary arenas in which God has placed us for service to others in this world:
   - family,
   - daily work,
   - religious institutions, and
   - engagement for the common good.

8. God gives us neighbors to serve in the primary community of family in which we are located for life. Two primary responsibilities of serving neighbors in families include the following:
   - providing basic nutrition, and
   - providing healthy nurture and solid education, leading to the capacity to care for others.

9. God gives us neighbors to serve in our daily work, no matter where that labor is lived out. Two primary responsibilities for serving neighbors in daily work include the following:
   - securing sufficiency for human livelihood, and
   - providing significance and meaning to life through the creative use of human gifts in the workplace.

10. God gives us neighbors to serve through religious institutions as these institutions contribute to the common good. Two primary responsibilities for serving neighbors through religious institutions include:
    - instilling a posture of gratitude in relation to life itself, and
    - promoting generosity in relation to the needs of others.

11. God gives us neighbors to serve through engagement for the common good. Two primary responsibilities for serving neighbors in public life include the following:
    - participation in the democratic process to implement strong and equitable laws that promote the good of all, and
    - community organization and advocacy in political process, not merely to guarantee one's own self-interest, but to protect the needs of "the least" (Matthew 25:31-46).

12. The rosters of the Evangelical Lutheran Church in America are each properly oriented in a theology of ministry that gives priority to equipping the baptized for neighborliness in daily life.

13. Diaconal ministers are called both to model through their own ministries and to foster among the baptized the fundamental movement from sanctuary to street, church to society, which is entailed in "the sending" from worship into the world.

14. Ordained ministers serve word and sacrament through preaching, teaching, worship leadership, and pastoral care, in order that the baptized are set free by the gospel of Jesus Christ *from* all that holds them captive and free *for* serving the neighbors whom God gives them in the four arenas of daily life.

15. Bishops serve the one, holy, catholic, apostolic church so that the ministries of unity (ecumenical relations, conflict resolution), holiness (discipline of faith and life), catholicity (global connections across time and space), and apostolicity (leadership in evangelical mission) promote the neighborliness of the baptized.

A missional ecclesiology orients all offices of ministry toward the sending of the baptized to be the primary agents in God's mission of serving neighbors in the world.

"One of them, a lawyer, asked [Jesus] a question to test him. 'Teacher, which commandment in the law is the greatest?' He said to him, "'You shall love the Lord your God with all your heart, and with all your soul, and with all your mind." This is the greatest and first commandment. And a second is like it: "You shall love your neighbor as yourself." On these two commandments hang all the law and the prophets'" (Matt. 22:35-40).

Having told his listeners the parable of the good Samaritan, Jesus asked: "'Which of these three, do you think, was a neighbor to the man who fell into the hands of the robbers?' He said, 'The one who showed him mercy.' Jesus said to him, 'Go and do likewise'" (Luke 10:36-37).

Being Lutheran Together in a Wider World

The old joke has been told in many variations. Someone dies and goes to heaven and is given a guided tour by St. Peter. At one point on the tour, they pass by a high, walled enclosure, and St. Peter gestures to his guest to tiptoe and keep silent. After the tour, the new arrival says, "St. Peter, there are so many beautiful neighborhoods in heaven, filled with such joy. But why did we have to keep quiet in that one part of heaven?" St. Peter responds, "Oh, those are the _____ [fill in the blank]. They think they're the only ones here."

The humor in the joke derives from the fact that many groups act like "the only ones here" already on earth. The writers in this section of *Together by Grace* remind us that we are *not* the only ones here, and that's very good news! We are part of communities gifted with rich differences—differences in ability, ethnicity, nationality, faith expression, and more. We are blessed to live in a time when we are not only aware of these differences but have many opportunities to dialogue, learn from, and build relationships with others. The 500th anniversary of the beginning of the Protestant Reformation is not a time to segregate ourselves in our own little corner but a time to embrace our presence in the richly diverse communities that are part of the world in which God has called us.

'No Longer Jew or Greek': Multiculturalism Has Pauline Roots

Alicia Vargas

The Pauline roots of Lutheran theology are as strong as they are well known. Most Lutherans have heard innumerable times, "For there is no distinction, since all have sinned and fall short of the glory of God; they are now justified by his grace as a gift, through the redemption that is in Christ Jesus . . ." (Rom. 3:22-24). Lutherans love the emphasis on grace.

Paul's emphasis on God's grace came out of a specific context. A few years after Jesus' death, Paul was already trying to make God's church multicultural. Many biblical passages reflect the first-century multicultural context. Take Pentecost: "And how is it that we hear, each of us, in our own native language?" (Acts 2:8). And Jesus' command to his disciples: Go make disciples "of all nations" (Matt. 28:19). Because Jesus' disciples obeyed his command, we are now Christians.

But Paul did more than talk about multiculturalism. He actively worked on transforming the early Christian community. Jesus and the first disciples were Jews. After Jesus' death some of the Jews who accepted Jesus as the Son of God insisted that all males had to be circumcised before they could join the community of Christ's disciples. "No!" Paul said. Not circumcision—God's grace and love justifies us and is the only necessary prerequisite to be a disciple of Christ. And that we have freely from God. We don't have to do anything to be "in" with God.

The Jewish men could follow their culture's expectation and be circumcised. The Gentiles didn't have to adopt the Jewish cultural ways. Both could

149

be Jesus' disciples. "Or is God the God of Jews only? Is he not the God of Gentiles also?" (Rom. 3:29). Just a few years after Jesus, the church already was multicultural.

One in Christ

Paul said, "There is no longer Jew or Greek, there is no longer slave or free, there is no longer male and female; for all of you are one in Christ Jesus" (Gal. 3:28). Not only is the body of Christ multiethnic (Jew or Greek) but also multiclass (slaves or free) and multigender (male and female). Paul says all of us are one in Christ. His vision of the church, the body of Christ on earth, was eminently multicultural in all sorts of ways.

The ELCA—which follows so passionately Paul's theology that insists on including all within Christ's body—is particularly called to continue in the Pauline tradition of *multiculturalism*. At its inception in 1988, the ELCA set a ten-year goal: The ELCA would be composed of at least 10 percent people of color in 1998. But in 2016 it's 3 percent people of color and 97 percent white.

The U.S. Census Bureau projects that the United States will have a majority of people of color in 2045, fewer than thirty years from now. The ELCA has a choice to make in view of those projections. Will it be a ghettoized church serving mainly the white minority in America in 2045 or will it be one with all the peoples and cultures in this land?

As important as diversity and representation are, more important is Jesus' mandate to share with "all nations" in America the Christian story and the special Pauline emphasis on grace.

Michael Aune, emeritus professor of liturgical and historical studies at Pacific Lutheran Theological Seminary, Berkeley, California, insistently reminded us that the Lutheran church in the United States has been multicultural since the boats started arriving from northern Europe. Germans and the various Scandinavians brought diverse Lutheran styles and traditions. Many years ago—and still today in some places—Lutherans worshiped in Finnish, German, or other languages. Then in 1988 three branches historically composed of those different ethnicities came together to form the ELCA.

But multiculturalism is a dynamic, contextual, and flexible social construct. Current U.S. multiculturalism isn't just composed of Germans, Scandinavians, British, Italians, and Irish. The number and power of other groups define our contemporary multiculturalism in America. Now we are mostly white, the cultural "melting pot" of earlier European immigrants. Those who will become the nation's majority in 2045 are Latinos, people of African descent, the many different Asian Americans and Pacific Islanders, American Indians, and many others. Some of these groups have been here as long as or longer than some white European immigrants and their descendants. But in terms of political power they were often invisible to the powerful majority and often more oppressed than now.

> **The U.S. Census Bureau projects that the United States will have a majority of people of color in 2045. . . . The ELCA has a choice to make in view of those projections.**

When we envision a multicultural ELCA we see our pews, pulpits, Sunday schools, council meetings, committee and task force meetings, synodical and churchwide administrative offices, seminaries, fiestas and potlucks, hands at work in the community—all that we are together—reflecting the country's diversity. I'm not talking about quotas or tokens. I'm talking about the full vision of the ELCA reflecting the fullness of the numbers and the gifts of all the people in the United States.

To reach this vision we need a lot of prayer, work, and self-reflection in our church. May God guide us in being one in Christ through and through.

Gifts and Tasks of Our Larger Lutheran 'We'

Kathryn Johnson

WHAT THE LUTHERAN WORLD FEDERATION MEANS FOR THE ELCA

ELCA members are accustomed to think about their local congregation, about their synod, and about the work of the national church. In addition to these expressions, though, through the Lutheran World Federation (LWF), they belong to a communion of 145 churches in the Lutheran tradition throughout the world. On behalf of 72 million people, almost 95 percent of the world's Lutherans, the LWF strives to address human suffering and injustice; to deepen relations among its member churches as they engage in all aspects of "holistic mission"; and to participate in dialogue with other Christian traditions and in collaboration with other faith groups while also developing Lutheran theological insights. In all these activities, the ELCA actively contributes and at the same time richly receives. While the LWF is not itself a church, it expands both experience and understanding of what it means to be Christ's body. At a time when global is a word of urgency and promise, the LWF deepens worldwide connections and provides a platform for common action.

As its name Federation still indicates, the LWF began in 1947 as a loose membership organization, with an emphasis on common response to needs in the aftermath of World War II. While that special attention to refugees remains important for the LWF, it has increasingly described its life as a journey to closer relationship, a "spiritual journey, where God's Spirit allows us to listen to one another and share our joys and sufferings" in "solidarity, interdependence and mutual responsibility." Experience with this common life prompted the LWF to declare itself a "communion of churches" in 1984, in part to support a call to accountability for those churches supporting the apartheid ideology in southern Africa.

More recently, this emerging identity has allowed the LWF to take crucial, communion-defining actions on behalf of its member churches together—actions that drew upon initia-

> **"**
> **The LWF deepens worldwide connections and provides a platform for common action.**
> **"**

tives in the United States and other local settings but then raised them to global significance and prominence. Two of these actions have been recognized as important not only for Lutherans everywhere but for the whole Christian church in its quest to heal its divisiveness.

- In 1999, the LWF and the Roman Catholic Church signed the *Joint Declaration on the Doctrine of Justification (JDDJ).* This common affirmation of God's gracious initiative recognized that on this topic so crucial to Lutheran beginnings the two parties no longer see the need to condemn one another's teachings.
- In 2010, the LWF Assembly publicly expressed its deep regret and sorrow over persecution of Anabaptists/Mennonites by Lutheran authorities, and especially over the theological support for this persecution offered by Lutheran reformers, which had remained unaddressed until our own time.

Together these actions have prepared the way for the extraordinary transformation in tone that marks the upcoming 500th anniversary of the Lutheran movement in 2017. In witness to transformed relationships, Pope Francis will join in inaugurating a year of "common commemoration" in Lund, Sweden—birthplace of the LWF—on October 31, 2016. This symbolic act builds upon the careful theological work of the *JDDJ* and the repentance of the 2010 "Mennonite action," which showed the renewal of spirit that can come from claiming the gifts of forgiveness and reconciliation. As LWF General Secretary Martin Junge said in announcing the Common Prayer in Lund, "I'm carried by the profound conviction that by working towards reconciliation between Lutherans and Catholics, we are working towards justice, peace and reconciliation in a world torn apart by conflict and violence."

Another important benefit of communion identity is the forum it provides for Lutheran churches together to experience the gifts of their rich diversities. Like all of world Christianity in recent decades, the LWF has experienced a shift in the balance of its membership toward the global South: the ELCA, the second-largest member church in the LWF as recently as ten years ago, is no longer among the largest five. To be sure, the ELCA engages partner churches around the world in many ways—from congregational initiatives, companion synod relationships, and the many activities of its Global Mission unit. Yet it is important that these bilateral relations are complemented by settings in which ELCA contributions enter into multi-lateral collaborations—in public witness on such issues as climate change, in service to the suffering, and in theological exploration. The Global Young Reformers Network and the Women on the Move project are two examples of opportunities to engage global diversity as 2017 approaches; joining in such projects as one important voice among many others is in itself an expanding experience. Through the LWF, the ELCA can augment its ministries beyond what is possible as a single church—and, in particular, as an American church, with the opportunities and burdens that identity brings.

The LWF speaks of communion, like other dimensions of Christian unity, as both "gift and task." The dimensions of gift—both from gratitude for God's grace and from the experience of relationship—are obvious and multiple. Yet communion is also task: if God's call is to the unity that honors difference, it is not possible to turn away from those relationships when the differences call for the hard, shared work of respectful listening. Questions around "who can be ordained?" for example, are answered in multiple ways among LWF member churches, and so far these churches have remained in communion. As such challenges and issues arise, the LWF provides places for shared worship and collaborative action which underline that the opportunity to engage difference is itself "gift," even when the "task" aspects seem more pressing.

As the ELCA looks to 2017 and beyond, it has much at stake in participating with the LWF in the ongoing work of self-definition for faithful witness in changing circumstances. Whatever changes or challenges arise, it can
fully affirm the vision its world body seeks to embody:

THE
LUTHERAN
WORLD
FEDERATION

**Liberated by God's grace, a communion in Christ
living and working together for a just, peaceful,
and reconciled world.**

**For more information about the Lutheran World
Federation, see http://www.lutheranworld.org.**

Ongoing Reformation: ELCA Ecumenical Relations

Kathryn Lohre

Historical context

In continuity with its predecessor church bodies, the Evangelical Lutheran Church in America came into being with a strong ecumenical self-understanding. The first Churchwide Assembly, in 1989, adopted *Ecumenism: The Vision of the Evangelical Lutheran Church in America*. This document provides a strong scriptural, confessional, and constitutional foundation for Lutheran ecumenism, based on Augsburg Confession VII, which reads: "For the true unity of the Church it is enough to agree concerning the teaching of the Gospel and the administration of the Sacraments" (*Ecumenism*, p. 9). *Ecumenism* also offers a history of the ecumenical strides made in the years leading up to the merger, as well as the ecumenical challenges inherited by the ELCA going back to the confessional polemics of the sixteenth century.

Importantly, *Ecumenism* notes that "the Lutheran Confessions were the products of an evangelical reform, which, contrary to its intention, resulted in divisions within the western church" (*Ecumenism*, p. 3). In the centuries that followed the Reformation, the intensification of global missionary efforts put the scandal of Christian division on display for the whole world to see. It is no coincidence that the launch of the modern ecumenical movement, the churches' quest for visible unity, at the 1910 World Missionary Conference in Edinburgh was unmistakably framed in terms of mission: "so that the world may believe" (John 17:21, NRSV).

The second ELCA Churchwide Assembly in 1991 adopted "A Declaration of Ecumenical Commitment: A Policy Statement of the Evangelical Lutheran Church in America." This policy has shaped our approach to bilateral dialogues, including our full communion partnerships and participation in councils of churches, and has provided a foundation for our inter-religious relations. The essence of this policy statement is that the ELCA is a confessional church that is evangelical, catholic, and ecumenical. In other words, we are committed to the gospel of Jesus Christ, the apostolic faith, and the oneness that is God's gift and calling to us. As we approach the 500th observance of the Reformation in 2017, the significant advances the ELCA has made in ecumenical and inter-religious relations can therefore be understood as part of the ongoing reformation of our church in today's rapidly changing religious landscape.

A brief overview of ELCA ecumenical relations

FULL-COMMUNION PARTNERS

The highest goal in ELCA ecumenical relations is that of full communion, when two denominations develop a relationship based on a common confessing of the Christian faith, a mutual recognition of baptism, and sharing of the Lord's supper. This is expressed through worship, evangelism, witness, and service in the world, and in many cases the exchange of clergy.

> **"**
> **We are committed to the gospel of Jesus Christ, the apostolic faith, and the oneness that is God's gift and calling to us.**
> **"**

The ELCA currently has four full-communion agreements, involving six partner churches.

After thirty-two years of Lutheran–Reformed dialogue in the United States, the ELCA, the Presbyterian Church USA, the Reformed Church in America, and the United Church of Christ entered into full communion in 1997. *A Formula of Agreement* describes a framework of mutual affirmation and admonition that has allowed the partner churches to explore deep areas of difference without division, including human sexuality.

In 1999, the ELCA entered into full communion with The Episcopal Church through *Called to Common Mission: A Lutheran Proposal for the Revision of the Concordat of Agreement.* This framework holds that "unity and mission are at the heart of the church's life, reflecting an obedient response to the call of our Lord Jesus Christ." This partnership is growing on the local level through clergy exchanges and cooperative ministries, and also as national staff counterparts develop new patterns of communication, coordination, and even shared positions.

The Methodist church in Germany is observing the 500th anniversary of the beginning of the Protestant Reformation with an image that includes five reformers: Martin Luther, John Calvin, John Wesley, Katharina von Bora Luther, and Ulrich Zwingli.

Also in 1999, the ELCA entered into full communion with the Moravian Church (Northern and Southern Provinces) as described in the agreement *Following Our Shepherd to Full Communion.* This formalized practices of partnership, clergy exchanges, and eucharistic hospitality that had been ongoing for decades. This relationship is thriving especially in areas with a strong Lutheran and Moravian presence, such as North Carolina and Pennsylvania.

In 2009, after thirty-two years of dialogue, the ELCA entered into full communion with the United Methodist Church. Over the years the dialogue focused on baptism, the role of bishops, and the Lord's supper, with interim eucharistic sharing put in place in 2004 as the final step before full communion. This agreement, *Confessing Our Faith Together,* marked the first time the ELCA had moved into a full communion relationship with a larger church body.

The reception, or living into, of each agreement is cared for by a coordinating committee. Each partnership is unique, with its own examples of joint mission and areas for growth. While common understandings of full communion tend to focus on the interchangeability of ordained ministries, the fullest and most innovative expressions of our visible unity in Christ tend to be those of joint mission.

BILATERAL DIALOGUE PARTNERS

Over the years, the ELCA's national and international bilateral dialogue partners have included the African Methodist Episcopal Church, the African Methodist Episcopal Zion Church, the Christian Church (Disciples of Christ), the Mennonite Church USA, the Orthodox Church, and the Roman Catholic Church. These dialogues are currently at varying stages of activity and progress. Each dialogue is intended to increase mutual understanding, heal wounds, and deepen relationships for the sake of Christian witness and mission.

Notably, the dialogues with two of the historic black churches in the United States (AME and AME Zion) have provided a strong foundation for seeking racial justice and reconciliation together, particularly in light of racially charged events, including the massacre of the Emanuel Nine in Charleston, South Carolina, in June 2015. The 2010 Statement of Mission adopted by the ELCA Conference of Bishops and the AMEZ Council of Bishops provides a strong basis for building local partnerships in dialogue and mission.

Dialogue with the Mennonite Church USA has focused on healing painful memories associated with the persecution of the Anabaptists by Lutherans and others in the sixteenth century. In 2006 the ELCA Conference of Bishops and Church Council adopted the "Declaration of the Evangelical Lutheran Church in America on the Condemnation of Anabaptists." In 2010, the ELCA participated in the actions of the eleventh assembly of the Lutheran World Federation—seeking forgiveness for the persecutions of the past, and looking toward the future as reconciled communities of faith.

In 2015, the ELCA together with the United States Conference of Catholic Bishops celebrated fifty years of Lutheran–Catholic dialogue. A task force of the two churches produced a new genre of ecumenical text, *Declaration on the Way* (Augsburg Fortress, 2016), which draws out thirty-two statements of agreement culled from the past fifty years of international dialogue reports on the topics of the church, ministry, and eucharist. As we look to 2017 and beyond we can point to ways in which Lutherans and Catholics are ushering in a new era of a common history and a commitment to the unity of the church. The 1999 Joint Declaration on the Doctrine of Justification provided a theological sign of this, while the anticipated joint ecumenical commemoration of the 500th observance to be held by the Lutheran World Federation and the Catholic Church in Lund, Sweden, on October 31, 2016, will provide a visible sign for the world to see, as Pope Francis and the leadership of the LWF join in common prayer and commitment to service.

CONCILIAR AND MULTILATERAL ECUMENICAL PARTNERS

In the United States and globally, the ELCA actively participates in ecumenical bodies, including the National Council of Churches (NCC), the World Council of Churches, Christian Churches Together in the USA, Church World Service, and Churches Uniting in Christ. The NCC's current priorities are inter-religious peacebuilding and opposing mass incarceration, taken up through four integrated areas of work: faith and order, justice and advocacy, education, and inter-religious relations. The tenth assembly of the World Council of Churches in Busan, South Korea, in 2013 called for a global pilgrimage for justice and peace, with strong witness on climate justice, overcoming violence and racism, and racial reconciliation. Organized into church families—Catholic, Evangelical, Pentecostal, Orthodox, African-American, and Protestant—Christian Churches Together in the USA focuses on prayer and fellowship and the possibility for a common public witness on major social issues, such as poverty, immigration, and racism. The ELCA is also active in Church World Service, which seeks to eradicate hunger and poverty and promote peace and justice, and in Churches Uniting in Christ, a multilateral body of churches that recognizes each other's ministries and seeks to combat racism in church and society.

As we look to the future, the ELCA faces three major ecumenical challenges: the challenge of reception, or living into our existing agreements and commitments; the challenge of deepening our existing partnerships; and the challenge of expanding our partners to include other churches. In an era of rapid change and increasing division, the ELCA's calling is to "strive toward fuller expressions of unity with as many denominations as possible" (*Ecumenism*, p. 4).

> *Ecumenism: The Vision of the Evangelical Lutheran Church in America*, **the ELCA's full communion agreements, and other documents and resources are available on the ELCA website at http://www.elca.org/Faith/Ecumenical-and-Inter-Religious-Relations.**

Ongoing Reformation: ELCA Inter-Religious Relations

Kathryn Lohre

Today, the quest for Christian unity is taking place amid unprecedented religious pluralism. The ELCA vision and policy statements on ecumenism adopted in 1989 and 1991 have provided an important foundation for our interfaith relationships as well as for our ecumenical commitments. As noted in the previous article, as we approach the 500th observance of the Reformation in 2017 the advances the ELCA has made in ecumenical and inter-religious relations can be understood as part of the ongoing reformation of our church in today's rapidly changing religious landscape.

The ELCA and its predecessor bodies have built a firm foundation in relationship with Jews and, more recently, Muslims. This was acknowledged in 1991 in "A Declaration of Ecumenical Commitment," which reads, "The Evangelical Lutheran Church in America does engage, in a variety of ways, in this inter-faith work and needs in the future a separate, official statement to describe its commitments and aspirations in this area" (*Ecumenism*, p. 13). Twenty-five years later, this work is a priority for ELCA Presiding Bishop Elizabeth Eaton.

Jewish relations

When the ELCA was formed in 1988 it inherited significant work in Jewish relations from its predecessor bodies, including years of global work through the Lutheran World Federation. Naturally, this became the initial focus of ELCA inter-religious relations. In the early 1990s, a Consultative Panel on Lutheran–Jewish Relations was established to increase cooperation with the Jewish community, to advance the conviction that anti-Semitism is "an affront of the Gospel, a violation of our hope and calling," and to live out our faith "with love and respect for the Jewish people." The panel invested its initial efforts in developing a document that would become central to our inter-religious life.

In 1994, acting under the mandate of the Churchwide Assembly, the ELCA Church Council adopted the "Declaration of the Evangelical Lutheran Church in America to the Jewish Community," rejecting Luther's later anti-Judaic writings, acknowledging their tragic effects throughout history, and reaching out in reconciliation and relationship to the Jewish community. The Jewish community received the Declaration with a great deal of appreciation, expressed in various ways. In Allentown, Pennsylvania, the Orthodox synagogue reached out to the Institute for Jewish–Christian Understanding at Muhlenberg College in a spirit of cooperation. The National Holocaust Museum in Washington, D.C., included mention of contemporary American Lutheran rejection of Luther's anti-Semitic views in one of its featured films. One of ELCA's Jewish dialogue partners and colleagues has a framed copy of the Declaration hanging on her office wall as a reminder of our commitments to her community.

In 2005 Rabbi Eric Yoffie, then president of the Union for Reform Judaism (URJ), addressed the ELCA Churchwide Assembly, the first Jewish leader and inter-religious guest to do so. He acknowledged his appreciation for "the role played by the [ELCA] in forging meaningful relationships between Christians and American Jews." This was in reference to the bilateral dialogue between the ELCA and the URJ, but also to longstanding local and national Christian–Jewish dialogues. Over the years, the consultative panel has developed resources in support of such dialogues for use in educational settings across the church.

Muslim relations

Luther also wrote troubling things about Islam in the context of the Ottoman Turkish advances in Europe. Nevertheless, while addressing difficult theological and pastoral questions about warfare and a possible crusade, he sought reliable information about Islamic teachings and insisted that Muslim Turks could lead virtuous lives—a useful precedent for today. In this vein, the ELCA and its predecessor bodies have nurtured a variety of relationships and participated in several initiatives with Muslims. In response to 9/11, the ELCA, like many other churches in the United States, committed to giving greater focus to Muslim relations, both bilaterally and through the national Muslim–Christian dialogue.

In 2007 the ELCA participated in responding to the global initiative "A Common Word Between Us and You"—an open letter from 138 Muslim leaders addressed to Christian leaders that underscored both religions' emphases on love of God and neighbor, and called for unity and peace on that basis. The following year, a group of ELCA scholars and leaders was convened to explore how the church could enhance its Muslim relations, becoming the Consultative Panel on Lutheran–Muslim Relations. Drawing upon the wisdom and experience of the Lutheran–Jewish Panel, this new panel set out to develop several resources to educate ELCA members and ecumenical partners on Islam and to nurture local dialogue and engagement, including "Talking Points: Topics in Christian–Muslim Relations." By the fall of 2010, Islamophobia had reached a fever pitch in light of the so-called Ground Zero Mosque controversy. Together with more than twenty interfaith partners, the ELCA became a founding member of the interfaith Shoulder to Shoulder Campaign: Standing with American Muslims, Upholding American Values, which sponsors an annual Emerging Religious Leaders Seminar, with active participation of Lutheran seminarians.

In 2011, on the tenth anniversary of 9/11, Dr. Sayyid Syeed of the Islamic Society for North America (ISNA) was the first Muslim speaker to address an ELCA Churchwide Assembly. He described how "during the last millennium mountains of hate [and] discrimination have been built." He said, "Our job is to see those mountains of hate removed." He was received by the assembly with a standing ovation. In August 2014 Presiding Bishop Elizabeth Eaton was invited, in turn, by Dr. Syeed to bring greetings to the Islamic Society of North America (ISNA) Convention in Detroit. The concerns raised by some ELCA members provided an opportunity to share information about the long-standing nature of our partnership with ISNA and our ongoing commitment as ELCA to Muslim relations.

Beyond the Abrahamic

The ELCA participates more broadly in inter-religious coalitions through bodies such as Religions for Peace–USA and the Council for a Parliament of the World's Religions, and in partnership with organizations such as the Interfaith Youth Core. Conversations have recently begun about possibilities for national ecumenical dialogues with other religious traditions, beginning with Hinduism and Sikhism. After the Oak Creek, Wisconsin, shootings in 2012, the ELCA was the first inter-faith partner to reach out, and a fledging relationship was established with Sikh leaders in the United States. In 2013 Tarunjit Singh Butalia of the World Sikh Council–America Region was the first guest from a *dharmic* tradition to address an ELCA Churchwide Assembly, where he thanked the church for this gesture of compassion.

> "
> *In partnership with our neighbors who share our concern for the common good, we find opportunities to collaborate for the sake of the world.*
> "

Expanding the table of our inter-religious partners must be done with careful attention to the reasons for doing so. There is a real concern that if we engage in inter-religious relations we are participating in a form of religious relativism, compromising our faith in Jesus Christ. Yet one of the learnings from inter-religious relations is that, in practice, precisely the opposite is true. By authentically engaging with others, we become more deeply grounded in who *we* are. In dialogue with others we are challenged to clarify what it is we believe, and why. In partnership with our neighbors who share our concern for the common good, we find opportunities to collaborate for the sake of the world. In other words, inter-religious relations both strengthen and support the Lutheran vocation. This is certainly true of the vanguard work in inter-religious understanding taking place on many ELCA college campuses.

In 2012 the ELCA Consultative Panels on Lutheran–Jewish and Lutheran–Muslim Relations met together for the first time to discuss how to shape the future for ELCA inter-religious relations in a way that is responsible to our Lutheran legacy and responsive to the rapidly changing multireligious context. In response, two of the ELCA's newest resources produced by the panels explore this question in depth: a pamphlet titled "Why Follow Luther Past 2017? A Contemporary Lutheran Approach to Inter-Religious Relations" (2014), which lifts up four of Luther's theological principles as instructive, and a book published by Lutheran University Press titled *Engaging Others, Knowing Ourselves: A Lutheran Calling in a Multi-Religious World* (2016), which explores real-life case studies of the practical and theological challenges facing Lutherans today. These projects are first steps toward building a framework for the future of ELCA inter-religious relations on the firm foundation that has already been established.

The intersection between ELCA Ecumenical and Inter-Religious Relations is one of the great challenges for the future. To have any real and lasting impact, the question of what it means to be Lutheran in a multireligious world must be explored in the context of what it means to be Christian in a multireligious world. In John 17:21, Jesus prayed "that they may all be one . . . so that the world may believe that you have sent me." Living this prayer is not a uniquely Lutheran challenge, but perhaps Lutherans have some unique insights to offer at the ecumenical table based on our history as well as our future directions. Our faithful witness to our unity in Christ, and our partnership with others for the sake of God's world, are part of our Lutheran vocation in a rapidly changing religious landscape—and a sign of our participation in the ongoing reformation as we approach 2017 and beyond.

The Challenge to Be an Authentically Multicultural Church

Albert Starr Jr.

More than twenty-five years into this journey together that we call the Evangelical Lutheran Church in America we find ourselves moving quickly toward the intersection of the observance of the 500th anniversary of the Reformation and what may well be some of the most racially turbulent times in this country since the "civil rights era" of the late 1950s and '60s.

We can celebrate that the relentlessly gracious presence of God is indeed constantly redeeming and renewing who we are as church. We can celebrate the good news and sacred promise that our God won't leave us alone. We can celebrate that our God is Emmanuel, with us always. We can, though I'm not sure just how much we do, celebrate that our God won't abandon us to be consumed by a diet of shallow celebration! We can celebrate that our God agitates and irritates in ways that reveal our real brokenness. We can celebrate that our broken places are where we can best see that precious grace of God at work in ways that make us even more who we really are.

Writers like Soong-Chan Rah remind us of the power of prophetic lamentation that "calls for justice in troubled times": "The crying out to God in lament over a broken history is often set aside in favor of a triumphalistic narrative. We are too busy patting ourselves on the back over the problem-solving abilities of the triumphant American church to cry out to God in lament."[1] We must be equally ready to acknowledge that, like generations of the church in society before us, much of our "diversity" may most honestly be measured in our broad range of readiness or lack of readiness for being a multicultural church with depth and integrity.

The meaning of multicultural

It does not serve us well to allow ourselves to slip into careless references to "multicultural" as meaning any congregation or context other than white. It is not honest for us to allow ourselves the presumed luxury of thinking that increasing the number of people of color on our membership rolls is consistently reflective of equitable sharing of power in matters of leadership and the continuous work of defining "Lutheran identity." It diminishes our true celebration of diversity to allow among us such narrow definitions of diversity that we have congregations and church leaders who say, "We're pretty much an all-white community; we don't have any diversity." The inability to recognize the wealth of diversity among us across socioeconomic, educational, and other cultural strata speaks volumes to the vast opportunity ahead of us as a church to truly deepen our capacity to recognize and value diversity across racial, ethnic, and other lines.

While we can celebrate the creating of ethnic-specific strategic plans adopted at Churchwide Assemblies, a number of social justice statements, and volumes of resources developed to help us as a church in our quest for becoming a truly multicultural church, we must confess that none of these tools will do the hard and demanding work for us. Ours is the work of building honest relationship as the beloved community. Covenant, in fact, is where we are perhaps most challenged as church, and that challenge is equally our greatest and most exciting frontier.

In 2015, in conversation with colleagues gathered in Kuala Lumpur, Malaysia, for the Asian Lutheran International Conference, it was clear as we reflected on where we were both in context and in the life of the church that we are being called toward real reformation in this twenty-first century. We were challenged: "Nowhere in the life of our church is the call for genuine reformation more evident than in our church's need for authentic engage-

---

1. Soong-Chan Rah, *Prophetic Lament* (Downers Grove, Ill.: InterVarsity Press, 2015), 68.

ment of people of color and people living impacted by poverty in every aspect of the life of our church."

To borrow from Old Testament scholar Walter Brueggemann, "We can along the way re-decide our notion of church. The covenant construct permits us and requires us to think afresh about the character and business of church."[2] We can celebrate standing on the cutting edge of experiencing our shared covenant relationship as the body of Christ more deeply than ever as we are agitated toward truth as God is incarnate among us in our relationship to one another. We can celebrate that our always present, agitating God will not leave us alone nor allow us the illusion that our true call is to anything but relationship.

Making the invisible visible

It has been a most debilitating part of our prevailing historical narrative as a church that people of color and people living in high-poverty circumstances are often seen more as recipients than resources. It is still painfully true in far too many contexts that our synods, church-related agencies and organizations, and congregations have not developed the depth of relationship with people of color that affords our church, in its many expressions, full opportunity to benefit from the passions, gifts, and capacity of people of color. It is an even more painful truth that

> **"**
> *We can celebrate that our always present, agitating God will not leave us alone nor allow us the illusion that our true call is to anything but relationship.*
> **"**

an untold number of people of color remain members of ELCA congregations but find themselves searching for engagement of their gifts outside the church. Still more tragic are instances where people of color are relegated to searching for their own authentic identity and sense of self, outside their church, apart from their faith because of narrowly defined, culturally bound notions of what it means to be Christian from a "Lutheran" theological or ecclesiastical perspective.

---

2. Walter Brueggemann, *The Covenanted Self* (Minneapolis: Fortress Press, 1999).

Yes, we celebrate the persons and places where the gifts and capacity of people of color are valued and involved in meaningful ways to further the mission, ministry, and life of the church, but we cannot afford illusions and false equivalencies. We celebrate the faithful engagement, and we lament the squandered opportunities to fully embrace and fully welcome.

Reports show that in the first ten years of the existence of the ELCA, from 1988 to 1998, the number of people of color who were active members increased in every ethnic community and category, while ELCA membership among European Americans declined over that same period. From 2009 to 2014 the number of active members who were people of color fell by an estimated 6.9 percent, compared to the church's overall 20.4 percent decline over what most would agree to be a tumultuous six-year period.

"When I heard these words I sat down and wept, and mourned for days, fasting and praying before the God of heaven" (Neh. 1:4). It was hearing the tragic condition of his people in peril that ushered Nehemiah into his prophetic role. When we hear the continuous reports of our church, the ELCA, declining and faltering in our call to be a church that reflects the holy vision of God's creative hand manifest in the diversity of God's people, will we just sit down, will we just mourn the prevailing report, or will we fast from the dictates of systems, structures, and budgets that nourish some while starving others?

Do we just want more reports that allude to progress we clearly know is yet to be attained, or will we step into the presence of the one who is able to do exceedingly and abundantly more than we can ask or imagine, to pray, *really pray*, knowing that to pray is to be changed. Like Nehemiah we are in a season that calls for more boldness than we've demonstrated, levels of investment that will draw on resources up to now left unengaged, and a willingness to go to some places we've only heard about from others.

Deciding to Choose

Nicole Newman

WORKSHOP WITTENBERG AND MY JOURNEY
TO CLAIMING MY LUTHERAN IDENTITY

In my life I have chosen many things: the college I would attend, the internships and jobs I would take, the friends I would have; and those choices have been important to me. More times than I have chosen things in my life, things have chosen me. These things have formed me, challenged me, and made me more of who I am than anything I could ever choose on my own.

I consider Lutheranism something that chose me. You see, I wasn't born Lutheran, and I came to the church after many years of being unconnected to any place of worship. In my congregation in Washington, D.C., there were people who kept reaching out, connecting with me, and giving me leadership opportunities. These people never pressured me to come to Sunday worship; they let me know that being a part of a community was more important than saying I was a member.

If the Lutheran church had waited for me to choose it, well, I am afraid I would not be writing this. Instead, the church was present, full of compassion for all of the complications and contradictions I brought. I was raised Baptist, I was a black woman, I was unsure of what I believed, and I was not convinced I wanted to be a part of a church that self-identified as a primarily white church. I had lots of questions and few answers I was sure of. The biggest gift of the church for me has been as a place to act on what I believed to be true about the world and put my values in action.

When I was nominated to be the North American delegate to represent the ELCA at Workshop Wittenberg, I found myself in a tension I had not anticipated. I was both excited and petrified. Two lingering questions for me were: Was I Lutheran enough? And what would this global community of young people I had never met expect an ELCA Lutheran to look like?

At this point, although I was active in both my local congregation and in some places in the national church, it was still mostly on my terms. I felt called to this church, and also felt I didn't quite fit. You see, although the church had chosen me, I wasn't quite ready to completely choose it back. I preferred a loose affiliation over commitment, but I boarded the plane hoping that, if nothing else, this experience would help me sort through whether I belonged. There was no better place to do that than in the place where students and scholars had gone before me. I wanted to see this Luther man, understand him better, wrestle with where I, in all my internationality, fit into the vision for the kin-dom of God. What I discovered has left me forever different.

What does it mean to be Lutheran?

The Workshop Wittenberg was a two-week international workshop hosted by the Lutheran World Federation (LWF) in 2015 for young Lutherans, as part of LWF's Global Young Reformers Network. The workshop afforded young people from all over the globe the opportunity to learn about Martin Luther and his experiences in the sixteenth century. We learned about his life and work and wrestled with questions about the church in our current time, in this current moment. We talked about what it meant to be Lutheran and be called to serve the world, what it meant to work ecumenically, and—most important—how to deepen our individual and collective understandings of the church in all its complexity and among varied expressions of the kin-dom of God.

I learned the Lutheran church is more than the context of the United States. There are culturally rich and vibrant congregations living and learning together in many places in the world. Having the opportunity to meet people from places I had never heard of challenged me to rethink what it meant to be a global citizen and what my responsibility was to pursue justice for the sake of the whole world, not just my corner of it.

The most important lesson was that being the church is not about one way of doing anything. Being the church is our commitment to how we are together in a world that is sometimes messy and confusing and mean. Sometimes when we talk about being one body it's easy to get raptured into a picture of harmony and peace. We think it's as simple as having a shared experience and glad hearts. There is a temptation for us to get lulled into the idea that conflict doesn't arise or, if it does, that it is always unhealthy. So we choose to be polite instead of honest. We want sameness, to believe the same things, to think the same way, to laugh at the same jokes, watch the same movies, or eat the same food.

But after two weeks living and learning and talking and eating and praying with people from all over the world, I have a more accurate picture. *Living* church instead of talking about it or trying to understand it makes things clear! Church is about people held together only by God's grace and their faith that God is in and among and working through them. That's a big thing to believe when language fails us or our own understanding is limited or we don't feel enough. Plus, being held together in relationship with our

> **The Global Young Reformers Network is a program of the Lutheran World Federation created by and for youth. We are active, creative young people who identify with their churches and therefore want to *reform* them. As we journey toward the 500th anniversary of the start of the Lutheran Reformation, we want to empower young people to engage in all aspects of church and communion life. With our global network of young reformers, we want to show the meaning of *ecclesia semper reformanda*—a church in ongoing reformation!**
>
> **The world is changing, and we as a Lutheran communion are called to act in response.**
>
> **Guided by Martin Luther's ideal of a church in ongoing reformation, we in the globalized world of the twenty-first century want to:**
> - **discuss what it means to be "Lutheran" today**
> - **create space to share our hopes and dreams**
> - **empower and equip young people to be reformers and to act boldly in faith, grounded in scripture.**

differences reflects how God creates each one of us in God's image. I cannot extend God's grace only to the people I agree with or who share my thoughts. God's love is truly for us all.

I also learned how much I don't like commitment. Being bound sounds hard to me—obligatory and like a mandate. Being in Wittenberg, I realized that the kind of being bound God invites us to comes from a place of freedom. It's a being bound that has a choice. I could run and hide behind what has always been done or I could come out and ask hard questions about race, about faith, and about life. I could be so tied to a belief that there is no place of possibility. I could decide that even though I was not a Luther scholar, I was Lutheran. I could choose this church because it was for me. If we say all are welcome, I had a choice: stand with one foot out and one foot in, or jump in and say that my mere presence in this church disputes the narrative that it is a white church. I could choose back. I could decide to listen to the voice of God calling me to be in full communion or keep pointing to the things that upset me as reasons I didn't belong.

> **Church is about people held together only by God's grace and their faith that God is in and among and working through them.**

It is our differences that allow us to depend on the grace of God. Workshop Wittenberg taught me to listen to understand, not to be right. I learned to engage from a place of authenticity and vulnerability and not to confirm what I already know (or think I know) to be true about the other. Most importantly, Workshop Wittenberg taught me that what I experienced in my congregation was possible in a larger context. God calls people together for reasons that are bigger than any of us may ever understand. The things we have in common or that are different can threaten to rip us apart, but they also have the potential to bring us together. We have a choice in the matter.

I am grateful to part of a church that doesn't rush to easy answers but sits in the tension of it all, constantly discerning how to choose love, choose Christ, and choose each other over and over.

Voices and Places: Stories from the Global Lutheran Family

In 1916, a book titled *Little Journeys with Martin Luther* was published anonymously. The plot of the book is that Martin Luther is brought back to life in the United States and goes about the task of trying to find a Lutheran church with which to affiliate. At the time, before the mergers of the early twentieth century, there were dozens of Lutheran bodies in the United States. Luther travels throughout the country, placed in scenes constructed by the author but speaking dialogue taken directly from his writings. Every Lutheran body existing at the time is either found unacceptable by Luther or finds Luther himself unacceptable. While the book is an enjoyable read, it is also a sad indictment of divisions among American Lutherans at the time. The problem *Little Journeys* highlights is not the differences as such; it's the inability or unwillingness of some to recognize others as really Lutheran.

That book was published on the eve of the 400th anniversary of the Reformation. The book you are holding in your hands is published on the eve of the 500th anniversary of the Reformation. While there are still divisions within Lutheranism, they are overshadowed by a growing recognition of and appreciation for the diversity within the Lutheran Christian family. Martin Luther's passionate insistence that the gospel message is "for you" is a theology that transcends place and time. In any and every context, this good news can take root in hearts and in lives. The Lutheran family—seventy-five million Christians in more than one hundred countries—incorporates many languages, cultures, and histories; yet all share a faith identity rooted in the Reformation witness to the gospel message of justification by God's grace through faith in Jesus Christ.

The authors in this final section of *Together by Grace* tell their own stories, offering a small but rich sampling of our common Lutheran family. Some are stories of suffering; some are stories of joy. All are stories of faith in the one "who for the sake of the joy that was set before him endured the cross . . . so that you may not grow weary or lose heart" (Heb. 12:2-3).

On Growing Up Christian in East Germany

Claudia Bergmann

Being a Christian in East Germany required a strong faith and a good amount of courage. Many East Germans today will tell you that going to church was illegal in the years between 1945 and 1989, but that was certainly not the case. The church as an institution was tolerated by the East German state and needed for its good connections to the West. Important events such as Martin Luther's 500th birthday in 1983 were celebrated so that appearances were kept up and tourist money could flow into the country. Luther even adorned an East German stamp. Yet the state employed other subtle and sometimes obvious means to make sure that religious observance was hindered, since religion was understood as the "opiate of the masses" and considered useless and old-fashioned.

One open way of eradicating the need for church was through replacing life-cycle events usually connected to church services, such as baptisms, confirmations, and funerals, with state-run substitutes. One example was *Jugendweihe* (youth dedication or consecration), a ceremony for fourteen-year-olds that was supposed to open the gate into adulthood. Schoolchildren would line up in festive clothes in a public space such as a theater, with their proud parents watching in the audience. They would listen to a state-sponsored speaker, promise to be true to their country, and receive a book that detailed what it meant to be a good East German citizen. After the ceremony they would receive gifts from their families and be called *Sie* by their teachers, the formal address in the German language given to esteemed adults. This substitute for the church's rite of confirmation is older than the East German state, but it took such hold in East German society that more than 90 percent of the children participated in it. A socialist naming ceremony that could be celebrated at the workplace and ceremonies at funerals were also offered, but they were much less successful.

The government used other, subtle means to create an atmosphere of oppression and fear among the Christian citizens of the country. Everyone knew that regular participation in a church service could invite a visit of the secret police, the Stasi. One could be denied the next step in one's career, a pay raise, or a place at the university for the children if one was known to be active in church. The state usually did not go after the people who were on the church membership rolls but generally inactive. But numerous eyewitnesses tell of the secret police taking photographs of people entering and leaving a church for worship services. There is ample evidence of pastors' houses being observed and bugged, church council members being questioned by the Stasi, participants in church-supported demonstrations for human rights or environmental concerns being imprisoned and mistreated. It was also common knowledge that pastors' kids would be denied further education unless, of course, the pastor worked with the secret police, which occasionally happened.

One person's story

My story touches on some of these issues. Born in 1969, I was baptized in the local church. As the fear and oppression among church members increased over the years, my parents did not want to subject themselves and me to that atmosphere. They simply stayed away from the church, except for Easter and Christmas services. They did not recommend that I go to Christian education classes, and as I got older they told me why. They too were afraid that I would be denied higher education. Thus, I participated in *Jugendweihe* with my peers. After that, and once it was decided that I would be allowed to go on to a high-school level at about age fifteen, I knocked on the pastor's door and asked to be confirmed and become an adult member of the church. A year of weekly classes followed during which I not only was taught the faith but also learned about the worldview of the church that often stood against what was taught in school and through official state channels. During that time, the story of the exodus from Egypt became important to me and many

Fall of the Berlin Wall, 1989.

others in the church, as we hoped that at some point we would be released from Pharaoh and live a life in freedom and without fear. My parents were never questioned by the Stasi when I started to attend church regularly and finally became confirmed, and neither was I. But at the time we received notice whether or not we were accepted into university, I realized that this step did have consequences for me. I was denied entrance into the university three years in a row. I finally gave up my dream of becoming a psychologist and decided to attend a church-run seminary to become a pastor. In 1989 I started my studies in Leipzig and studied Greek and Latin in the morning while at night attending the demonstrations that, in the end, led to the downfall of East Germany.

Right after I started, I received a letter from the university telling me that they suddenly had a place for me, but by that time, my mind was made up. I was never again to be manipulated in my decisions by the socialist

> **"**
> *Because of the socialist state's actions against the faith and the church, being a Christian . . . still poses a challenge.*
> **"**

state. Fortunately, I was never imprisoned for printing illegal newspapers in Leipzig or beaten for attending the 1989 demonstrations, as many of my peers were.

Many years later, as a pastor in Luther's hometown of Eisleben, I realized that the socialist state that had caused so much fear during my youth had in many ways succeeded. Few church members attended church; they had become accustomed to not participating and being quiet about their Christian faith. Among the younger generations, there was and is little knowledge about the church and its teachings. As the grandparents had decided to leave the church because of fear and oppression, they had not transmitted the faith to their children and subsequently their grandchildren. The church in East Germany is, in my eyes, a mission field where the institution has to regain trust, and the stories of the faith have to be told again and anew. There are still people here who have never stepped into a church, have no idea what the cross symbolizes, and do not know the meaning of Christmas and Easter. Because of the socialist state's actions against the faith and the church, being a Christian almost three decades after the Berlin Wall came down still poses a challenge. But it's a challenge that might lead to a new beginning.

A Brief History of the Evangelical Lutheran Church in Guyana

Winston D. Persaud

A PERSONAL REFLECTION ON THE POWER OF THE GOSPEL OF JESUS CHRIST IN A POST-COLONIAL SETTING

The story of the birth of the Evangelical Lutheran Church in Guyana (ELCG), the oldest church in Guyana (earlier known as Guiana), evokes surprise and curiosity. On October 15, 1743, a group of Dutch planters met in the home of planter Lodewyk Abbensetts and decided to found a church of the "unaltered Augsburg Confession" of 1530. That Lutheran congregation began about eighty-five miles up the Berbice River. The ELCG's 270th anniversary, in 2013, was marked by commemorative postage stamps in Guyana.

My Indo-Guyanese family's story reflects the wider history of Guyana, for their presence in the former British colony—acquired in the early 1800s and granted independence on May 26, 1966—is tied to the end of slavery in the British West Indies in 1838 and the consequent importation of indentured servants from India, which began that same year. I am a second-generation Christian whose roots in the Lutheran heritage are grounded in the broader economic, religious, ethnic, and cultural history of Guyana and other countries in the British Empire. When my parents were married in 1949, my mother was a Hindu and my father a Christian convert from Hinduism, baptized in 1944 before he left for England to serve in the Royal Air Force during World War II. In their arranged marriage, the tacit understanding between my parents was that my mother would not be forced to become a Christian to please my father and that the children born in the marriage would be brought up as Christians in the Lutheran church, in which my father's eldest brother was a catechist.

> "
> *Today ELCG membership reflects Guyana's ethnic-racial diversity. This evangelical turnaround is an expression of the priesthood of all believers.*
> "

By 1838, British Guiana (formerly three colonies ruled by the Dutch since the early 1600s) had experienced Christian communities for almost two hundred years, and there was now a diversity of Christians. In addition to Anglicans, Church of Scotland Presbyterians, Roman Catholics, Congregationalists, Moravians, and Methodists, there were Lutherans, exclusively in Berbice. In the 1930s, Epiphany Lutheran Church became the first Lutheran congregation in Georgetown. It is a poignant reality that by the dawn of the twentieth century the churches reflected in varying degrees the minority northern European population, Africans (former slaves and the largest population group), those of mixed race, Portuguese, Chinese, American Indians, and a small number of East Indians. East Indians were primarily Hindu, with a significant Muslim minority and a few Christians among them. Between World War I and World War II and later, through the building of schools and learning how to reach out to the East Indians on the sugar plantations, Lutheran church membership (along with that of Canadian Mission Presbyterians, Anglicans, and Methodists) began to include the East Indians. Today ELCG membership reflects Guyana's ethnic-racial diversity. This evangelical turnaround is an expression of the priesthood of all believers, for in 1743 the church was for Dutch planters only, with no evangelical outreach or openness to the African slaves or indigenous peoples.

The ELCG's symbol of a swan, the cross, and Bible has its origin in the church's Dutch founding. The meaning of the cross and Bible is self-evident: salvation through Christ alone, and scripture alone. The tradition of the swan is intriguing. It symbolizes Luther, whose coming had been predicted by Jan Hus when the latter was burnt at the stake on July 6, 1415. On that fateful day, the tradition goes, Hus declared, "You may roast this goose, but in a hundred years a swan will arise whose voice you will not still."

Through the visionary work of the first Guianese pastor, the Rev. John Robert Mittelholzer (1878–1913), Lutheran missionaries, ordained and lay, came from the United States and Canada. Today Guyanese pastors and lay leaders, accompanied by partners in the global church, particularly in North America, continue to bear witness to the gospel of Jesus Christ.

A Church Alive in the Spirit

Kristin J. Wendland

THE ETHIOPIAN EVANGELICAL CHURCH-MEKANE YESUS

There were people as far as we could see. On a hot weekend in March 2011, nearly ten thousand people had gathered to celebrate the fiftieth anniversary of the Central Synod of the Ethiopian Evangelical Church–Mekane Yesus (EECMY). The two-day celebration included sermons, a large choir, a solo singer from Addis Ababa, greetings from international companions, and a healer, whose ministry was marked by healings and people in the crowd speaking in tongues and being slain by the Spirit. This was the Lutheran church as I had not experienced it before.

I was a guest of EECMY's Central Synod. The ELCA's La Crosse Area Synod had had a companion synod relationship with the Central Synod for twenty years. As part of that relationship, two EECMY pastors had traveled to the United States to teach in congregations, and I was the eleventh "teaching pastor" traveling from the

> **"**
> *This was the Lutheran church as I had not experienced it before.*
> **"**

La Crosse Area Synod to teach at the Nekemte Christian Education College, a seminary three hundred kilometers from Addis Ababa. I taught my students the basics of biblical Greek and pastoral care, and they taught me about their way of being church.

My students pointed to Acts 8, where Philip baptized the Ethiopian man he met alongside the road, as the beginning of Christianity in Ethiopia. The roots of the EECMY, however, go back to Swedish missionary activity in the first half of the twentieth century. Since its formation in 1959 the EECMY has experienced tremendous growth. According to the EECMY website, at the end of 2014 the baptized membership of the EECMY was 7.4 million. Through personal communication, an EECMY leader shared that this number had grown by nearly 85,000 in 2015. With only 8,360 pastors and evangelists in the church, much of this growth is due to individuals witnessing to Christ in their daily lives.

Ethiopian in character

While the Swedish Lutheran influence continues to be seen in aspects of the liturgy and the architecture of the church buildings, the EECMY is thoroughly Ethiopian. Praise choruses and spontaneous prayer punctuate the weekly three-hour-long worship services. Double-wide pulpits allow for services to be conducted in multiple languages. Youth and mission conferences regularly draw thousands of people. To accommodate the large and growing number of people attending worship each Sunday, open-air porches flank the

sides of most buildings, and children often stand outside, their arms hanging inside the open windows.

The tagline of the EECMY is "Serving the Whole Person." To live this out, the church has a robust social service program. It manages health clinics, mobile health units that travel to rural areas, food and clothing programs, housing programs for those who have lost parents due to the AIDS epidemic, agricultural programs, and other services through its Development and Social Service Commission.

In its relatively short life, the EECMY has been marked by persecution. During the communist Derg regime consolidated under Mengistu Haile Mariam (1974–1991), EECMY congregations were technically permitted to continue meeting as long as members did not publicly witness to their faith. A number of church leaders were imprisoned, and gathering for worship or prayer became a dangerous activity. The church, nonetheless, continued to grow. Religious tensions remain high in the country, where large groups of Orthodox Christians, Muslims, and Protestant Christians live alongside one another.

All these things—lively and Spirit-filled worship, a commitment to serving physical as well as spiritual needs, and a living memory of persecution—are part of what characterize the EECMY as it continues to live and grow in Jesus' name.

Hope: From Being Wives of the Pastors to Being the Pastors

Paulina Ewa Hławiczka

I never really wanted to be a pastor, as others wanted me to be. I was born in southern Poland to a family that was Lutheran from the time of the Reformation, a family that brought to the world plenty of pastors and artists. I always dreamed to be a part of the second group, an artist. Thus began a lifelong process in which various emotions like frustration and despair fought against, and were finally conquered by, another force that comes from God: Hope.

God led me in another direction, and it caused some strong questions within me. I bargained with God. I said, "Okay, you pushed me to study your subject, so allow me to study mine too!" Hope.

Some tutors at the theological academy didn't approve my wanting to study opera. They said I should know what God called me for. But this is how my parents introduced me to the church—through music! There were only two places available in the opera school and a huge number of competitors. When I was awarded the first place, I knew this was God's answer to our haggling. As promised, I finished my theological studies with a master's diploma about hope. Both courses of study, theology and opera, were very exciting and I was blessed in many ways, but I had to earn money as well as study. I had my dark moments, and I thought it was wrong to bargain with God.

In Poland, when you are at the end of theological training the bishop calls you to have a conversation about your future. Hope.

The bishop asked me why, during my five years of theological study, I didn't find a husband, another theologian who would be a pastor soon? It would be much easier for them if I had one! They could send me with him to his new parish and let me do some volunteer services, or, if lucky, find a job at a school. Without a husband he could only offer me to be a cleaner at the church, he said with a funny smile.

I'd been fighting for human rights and women's rights against the bishop's office before, so I took it as revenge. At that point, the only thing I wanted was to leave the church and focus solely on music. But then I received a job offer from the army chaplaincy in the Ministry of Defense, where I became personal assistant to the military bishop and later also co-editor of the military magazine. Hope.

> **Hope teaches us how to care for the good, how to fight for our rights, how to educate children and young people for a better world.**

Fighting for women's rights was still a daily responsibility, but many times it was fruitful. In addition, I was offered the opportunity to perform as a singer for soldiers and commanding generals in the Ministry of Defense. I could combine my theological and musical gifts again. However, my father's death shadowed my little success. This event was followed by other deaths: the 2010 plane crash with the Polish president on board, in which we lost one hundred government leaders, and I lost my closest friend. As one of the leaders of the crisis staff after this tragic accident, I couldn't leave my position for many long months. When I finally left, I was very ill and weak, needed hospitalization, and nearly died during an operation. When I woke up in 2011, I found myself among family, friends, and my spiritual mentor. Hope.

I wasn't fully recovered when I was called to work for the Polish Ecumenical Council and lead two projects for them. Hope.

Then I was accused of writing libel about the bishop of the church. Happily, the real writer confessed. Nevertheless the incident made more enemies for me, and I wasn't allowed to work for the council any longer.

I planned journeys, first to Germany, then to England, to recover and spend some time abroad with distant family and new wonderful friends I had met through the work with the Polish Ecumenical Council. Hope.

Although I definitely longed for a break from the church and from work, and began to miss my country, I stayed in Britain and became involved in church matters again almost unconsciously, until it was too late to say: "Wait a minute! I've planned a break from the church!"

Today I am pastor in charge of two congregations in two different English towns: Nottingham and Corby. I am also one of seven directors of the council of the Lutheran Church in Great Britain. All our pastors are contracted part time and need a second job to survive. For the British Lutheran church to ordain me, the first criterion was to have a second profession. Finally I could say without any fear—and I could believe it!—that I am a classical singer. Hope.

It is not easy to pray and preach in a language that is not your mother tongue. But what a challenge to learn all the new skills, to meet new people, to speak up without the fear that someone will punish you soon because you are a woman! Hope.

My involvement in the movement to aid Polish women theologians continues. It is stronger and from a different perspective now. The Polish church invites me to share lectures, stories, sermons, and opinions. Hope.

Hope teaches us how to care for the good, how to fight for our rights, how to educate children and young people for a better world. Hope gives us a warmer attitude toward others, and it helps us to trust God, to make our ideas about God bigger and wider. Through hope, we make new steps and new ways.

"Even if I knew that tomorrow the world would go to pieces, I would still plant my apple tree" (attributed to Martin Luther).

 'I Am a Palestinian Christian'

Mitri Raheb

I was born in Bethlehem on June 26, 1962, into a family that took root in this city a very long time ago. The Raheb family has lived in and around Bethlehem for many centuries. This small and in some ways insignificant city has, in the course of history, attained worldwide renown. It was here around 1000 BCE that David was born, out of the tribe of Jesse, later to become the anointed king of Israel. But Bethlehem's particular claim to historical fame is that it was the birthplace of Jesus the Christ. It was through him that "Bethlehem of Ephrathah, who are one of the little clans" (Micah 5:2) became "by no means least among the rulers of Judah" (Matt. 2:6).

> **"**
> *The attempt is to take two steps into the daylight of the future even though we are still standing in the darkness of the present.*
> **"**

My identity was stamped by the fact that I was born in this particular place. I feel I have something like a special relationship to David and to Christ—a relationship developed not only by way of the Bible, not only through faith, but also by way of the land. I share my city and my land with David and with Jesus. My self-understanding as a Christian Palestinian has a territorial dimension. I feel that I am living in a continuity of locale with these biblical figures, sharing the same landscape, culture, and environment with them.

Near the end of the 1970s, I had just finished my high school education and had decided to study theology. One of my friends came to see me and asked me whether I thought it made sense to study theology. He told me, "By the time you finish your studies, there will be no Christians left in Palestine. They will all have emigrated. The many churches of the Holy Land will have been transformed into museums, and you will be unemployed unless you work as a museum guide. But you don't need to study theology to do that."

I listened to his words with great sorrow, for I knew that he was not talking nonsense. More and more Palestinian Christians were leaving the Holy Land. They left their home and that of their ancestors to try their luck somewhere else; anywhere, where life is calmer, more peaceful, and more stable.

One of the greatest challenges confronting the Palestinian Christian today is emigration. Many have started to ask seriously whether there will be any native Christians left in the Holy Land in the near future, whether this country will become a kind of Christian Disneyland

On January 29, 2016, the Rev. Dr. Mitri Raheb and Israeli journalist Gideon Levy received the Olof Palme Prize in Stockholm, Sweden, "for their courageous and indefatigable fight against occupation and violence, and for a future Middle East characterized by peaceful coexistence and equality for all." In his acceptance speech Pastor Raheb pointed to the significance of the year 2017: it is the one hundredth anniversary of the Balfour Declaration, in which the British government expressed its support for Palestine as a homeland for the Jewish people, and also the fiftieth anniversary of the occupation of the West Bank, the Gaza Strip, and the Golan Heights by Israel.

In his acceptance speech, Raheb said:

As a pastor who lives in the little town [of Bethlehem], I keep asking myself: how will our people survive, physically, socially, economically, and spiritually? How can I preach the good news for people who wake everyday just to hear another bad news? . . .

We are not only denied our political and economic rights, but also our cultural and religious rights. We are denied the right to have our own narrative that stands on its own; the right to tell our story the way we experience it; the right to read the Bible with our own eyes and not always with a Eurocentric post-Holocaust lens. . . . As a Christian theologian, I have to say that it is not acceptable to violate human rights in the name of divine rights, or to play God against the humans. No religion is entitled to give the Israelis more rights than Palestinians, Muslims more privileges than Christians, or men higher wages than women. Equality is something we cannot compromise on.

or theme park, and whether all that will remain here to visit and admire will be heaps of stones which have ceased being witnessing, "living stones."

In 1988, encouraged by the Palestinian National Council's Declaration of Independence of the State of Palestine, I dared to dream a dream. This dream of a "two-states solution" is not an ideological concept, not a rigid structure, and not definitive. It is well known that dreams have no boundaries. Nor should this dream have a rigid boundary; it is a dream that can still be dreamed, but it also cries out for a greater dream. The most important question is still: Does this dream have the strength to set something in motion? Will it remain a pious wish or will it make history?

The "separation wall" between Israel and the Palestinian Territories, seen from the roof of the Wi'am Palestinian Conflict Resolution Center in Bethlehem.

Some years have passed since I dreamed the dream. I hope it is not out-dated; it was already a daring risk at the time because, as I said then, "The attempt is to take two steps into the daylight of the future even though we are still standing in the darkness of the present."

I am a Palestinian living under Israeli occupation. My captor daily seeks ways to make life harder for me. He encircles my people with barbed wire; he builds walls around us, and his army sets many boundaries around us. He succeeds in keeping thousands of us in camps and prisons.

Yet despite all these efforts, he has not succeeded in taking my dreams from me. He could not imprison them. His suppression could not keep me from thinking of a joint future with him. His brutality against the Intifada did not succeed in discouraging me from dreaming of a peaceful coexistence with him. I have a dream that I cherish and care for like my own child.

I have a dream of two peoples who are not separated by a wall. The Berlin Wall is already past history. The time of the Cold War is over—I hope not only in Europe and the Northern Hemisphere. A truce and small wars no longer satisfy us. What both peoples need is peace: a real, just, and true peace.

A Witness of a Lutheran Christian Dalit Woman in India

Nelavala Gnana Prasuna

Untouchability, subordination, marginalization, disparities, exploitation, deprivation, and discrimination are the common features of Dalit life, especially for Dalit women. The Dalits are those regarded as "untouchable" in the Hindu caste system. Beginning in the nineteenth century, Christian missionary activity helped provide education and employment opportunities that increased their status and identity in society.

Story of the South Andhra Lutheran Church

Like many other churches in India, the South Andhra Lutheran Church (SALC) came into existence through missionary intervention. The Rev. August Mylius, from the Hermannsburg Evangelical Lutheran Mission in Germany, arrived in Andhra Pradesh in 1865 and baptized a man named Rangayya along with his two children. This was the beginning of what would become the South Andhra Lutheran Church, which now has a history of 150 years. The SALC was under the Hermannsburg Evangelical Lutheran Mission from 1865 to 1914, under the Ohio Evangelical Lutheran Mission from 1920 to 1929, and under the American Lutheran Church from 1930 to 1941.[1] Only after Indian Independence in 1947 did the church come to be independent and known as the South Andhra Lutheran Church.

---

1. The gap between 1914 and 1920 was due to the interruption of German missionary activity by World War I. American Lutherans took up many of the overseas missions the Germans were forced to abandon at the end of the war.

Missionaries (forty-seven male and twenty-eight female) have done tremendous work toward the transformation of the community of Dalits. They
established schools, hostels,
orphanages, old-age homes,
hospitals, industrial schools,
and Bible training schools for
men and women. As a result
of this missionary work, Dalit
Christian men and women in
the southern parts of the state

> **"**
> *My great grandparents were
> 'no people.' But a drastic shift
> from 'no people' to Christian
> community took place with the
> conversion of my grandparents.*
> **"**

of Andhra Pradesh had access to education that paved their way for employment and thus have the benefit of a better status when compared to Dalit
people of other religions. My story is a witness to that transformation.

My story

I am a third-generation Christian woman born into a home that was rooted
in Lutheran Christian faith. I was raised in a middle-class socio-economic
setting as my parents are teachers. Currently, I am married and I have two
sons. Both my spouse's education and my own allow us to lead a fairly
middle-class lifestyle.

My experience as a Dalit Christian Lutheran woman is essential for how
I do theology.

My great grandparents were "no people." But a drastic shift from "no people" to Christian community took place with the conversion of my grandparents. My grandmother, my father's mother, was not able to bear a child even
after ten years of her marriage. She heard the gospel and believed in Christ, and
on one fine day she was surprised to find that she had conceived. She delivered
her firstborn son and named him Devashayam, which means "God's help."
She then received baptism, and her entire family also received baptism. My
mother's parents, cousins of my father's parents, also converted to Christianity,
and when they gave birth to a baby girl they named her Devadanamma, which
means "God's gift." Since then a great change happened in their lives and in
their villages as well, as their children were sent to mission schools and were
educated and acquired a more dignified level of existence.

Being teachers, my parents rented houses in the main villages, and we
lived among the caste people—those who had status in the Hindu caste

The Rev. Dr. Nelavala Gnana Prasuna, a Lutheran, is academic dean of Mennonite Brethren Centenary Bible College in Telangana, South India. She is shown here posing with a tree planted in the Luther Garden in Wittenberg, Germany, by the Mennonite World Conference.

system. Thus, to a great extent we escaped the stigma of untouchability that is the customary attitude toward Dalit Christians. Christmas and birthday celebrations were great occasions for us to invite our neighbors to dine together and also to share the gospel. At the same time, we were also invited by them to participate in their special ceremonial celebrations.

My parents were government employees, so we enjoyed relatively improved economic status. We are four in our family, and all of us were well educated. In the whole SALC, only two men and two women have earned doctorates in theology, and my sister Nelavala Surekha and I are among those four! That is witness to the transformation that took place for Dalits in the SALC.

Most of my childhood was spent in rural villages where the caste system was predominant. As there were no churches in villages, our home would be turned into a church, as my parents conducted Sunday worship services. As children we were nurtured in Christian faith. We used to have regular family prayers both in the morning and evening. Our parents taught us to have regular personal devotions. My early childhood experiences of faith, of confrontation with the caste system, and of improved socioeconomic status have been significant for me in my self-understanding and in articulating theology. However, it is clear that my story is not the story of many women in Indian society and the church. Women continue to face violence and suffer disadvantages and live underprivileged lives. Too many Christian women still suffer due to traditional and oppressive interpretations of the scriptures and theology.

Out of the Depths
I Cry to You

Heidi Michelsen

There I was, all alone in a Salvadoran jail. A soldier had taken away my tiny Gideon Bible, so all I had left for comfort was what any cradle Christian has after a lifetime of Sunday school, Bible study, and worship: Bible texts I had memorized, hymns, the liturgy, the Lord's Prayer. It was October 31, 1989, and I knew that at that moment someone somewhere in the world was probably singing "A mighty fortress is our God." I was crazy with worry about my own death, thinking I might well end up like the four U.S. Catholic churchwomen who had been raped and murdered in El Salvador in 1980. So I reached within my memory and out popped that old Reformation song. I sang verses one and two, and then continued with verse 3,

> Though hordes of devils fill the land, all threatening to devour us,
> we tremble not, unmoved we stand; they cannot overpower us.
> Let this world's tyrant rage; in battle we'll engage!
> His might is doomed to fail; God's judgment must prevail!
> One little word subdues him.

In the past I had wanted to dismiss this verse, with its medieval, seemingly outdated worldview. But somehow, there in the belly of the beast, it was this verse that was the most comforting. Because in that moment I didn't need a cute, sweet, meek baby Jesus. I needed a strong advocate, up to doing battle with the evil principalities and powers, powers that were, at that very moment, torturing some poor soul in the next cell whose only crime may have been belonging to a union, participating in a small Bible study group, or working as a literacy teacher. I needed the "chase the moneychangers out of the temple" Jesus, a Christ who could kick the pants out of the human evil in that place. I thought about Luther, there in Wartburg Castle, not knowing what his fate might be, but having made his stand, clinging to this strong Jesus for dear life.

Many Lutherans I know from Central America seem to identify more with the witness of Luther's life than the doctrine of justification by faith. It's not that they don't believe in justification by faith; indeed they do. But they are less interested in the hereafter than the here and now—in a world wracked with hunger, war, and climate change, in which they must face the impossible choice of either watching their children threatened and killed by powerful gangs, or sending them, like Moses's mother did, off in a basket down the river to an unknown place—in this case to Costa Rica or the United States. So they can identify with Luther's courage in the face of death threats from church and empire, and they remember that if it hadn't been for the creative genius of Luther's friends in having him "kidnapped" he may have ended up a martyr just like the Czech reformer Jan Hus. The situations they face demand the same kind of creativity and commitment.

> **"**
> *In times of crisis and violence, what keeps one going is the support of the Christian community and a lively hope in the resurrection.*
> **"**

In times of crisis and violence, what keeps one going is the support of the Christian community and a lively hope in the resurrection. It's as if we need to grab that justification promise with both hands and pull it from the future to the present, to give us strength for the journey today, for the daily battles against all the powers of death. For some that means strength to face the challenges of everyday life: cancer, broken relationships, addictions, whatever. For others it may require strength to risk even their very lives for the sake of justice and building more perfect expressions of the kingdom of God, here on earth as in heaven, just like brother Martin did so long ago.

Breaking Bread Together in Namibia

Nancy Larson

Namibia gained its independence from South Africa in March 1990. While it is young as an independent nation, it has a long and deep history. The name comes from the Namib Desert, which comprises a large part of the country's landmass and is believed to be the oldest desert on the face of the earth.

The Lutheran church in Namibia has a long history with missionary movements from Germany and Finland, among others; the Lutheran presence dates back more than 150 years. A country now estimated to be 90 percent Christian and 60 percent Lutheran, Namibia can teach us much about evangelism and church growth. Since achieving independence, Namibia has made strides in economic development, expansion of its education system, and resource management. Yet it still faces significant challenges with a 40 percent unemployment rate, the HIV/AIDS pandemic, and malaria and tuberculosis among the toughest.

The current state of the Lutheran church in Namibia is complex and amazing. It is made up of three different church bodies: the Evangelical Lutheran Church in the Republic of Namibia (ELCRN), the Evangelical Lutheran Church in Namibia (ELCIN), and the *Deutsche Evangelisch-Lutheranische Kirche* (DELK), or German Evangelical Lutheran Church. The relationships among these church bodies bear the scars from years of pre-independence strain to this day. The challenge to these relationships is derived from each church body's own history and how they understood themselves in the context of their national identity.

The Evangelical Lutheran Church in the Republic of Namibia is based predominantly in the southern three-quarters of Namibia. It was established primarily through German missionary outreach to the indigenous Namibian peoples beginning in the early nineteenth century. Its congregations reflect that northern European connection. As the efforts for Namibian independence gained strength, the leadership and members of the ELCRN lent their efforts to prayer and diplomatic initiatives, seeking a nonviolent means for establishing an independent Namibia, defeating South African rule, and bringing an end to the injustice of the apartheid system.

The Evangelical Lutheran Church in Namibia works predominantly in the northern quarter of Namibia. This church was born of the efforts of Finnish missionaries to bring Christ to the native population, also in the nineteenth century. These congregations reflect their Nordic roots. In the case of the ELCIN, the battle for independence took a more proactive approach, with leaders and members working more directly with freedom fighters, providing refuge, more direct assistance, and even at times taking up arms alongside them. They believed that if they wanted to be independent they needed to put themselves and even their lives on the line.

The *Deutsche Evangelisch-Lutheranische Kirche,* or German Evangelical Lutheran Church, was established by those who came from Germany to claim and settle the land. They established ranches and farms and became the ruling landowners. This church is still basically a part of the Evangelical (Lutheran) Church in Germany (EKD), which sends pastors and bishops from Germany to serve the congregations throughout the country. By far the smallest of the church bodies, they worked against an independent Namibia.

Past struggles, future hope

It should be no surprise, then, that these three church bodies have struggled with how to relate to one another in an independent Namibia. They have looked upon one another with mistrust and skepticism. That is why an invitation to be part of the first ever official consultation with the three Namibian churches was received with humility and honor. I represented the Northeastern Iowa Synod, along with representatives of the New Jersey Synod, the Metro Washington, D.C., Synod, and the Southwestern Washington Synod (the four ELCA synods with companion synod relationships to Namibia). ELCA Global Mission staff were an important part of the planning and financial support for this consultation. We traveled to Windhoek, Namibia, in the spring of 2005 to spend four days in Bible study, conversation, covenant development, and breaking bread together. I was asked to lead the opening Bible study on Luke 24:13-33. This road to Emmaus text provided a wonderful means of generating conversation about God in our midst as we too journeyed together. In the breaking of bread we came to see a new path for moving forward together in mission and ministry. The consultation concluded with the approval of a formal covenant of relationship among the three church bodies by all present and gathering together around the Lord's table.

> **"**
> *In the breaking of bread we came to see a new path for moving forward together in mission and ministry.*
> **"**

This historic gathering accomplished more than anyone had hoped or dreamed. A United Church Council was established with representatives from all three church bodies. They began to work together to find ways to support one another in ministry and share programs and projects. This joint council was commissioned in the spring of 2007 in another historic gathering with partners from Finland, Germany, the Netherlands, Norway, and the United States. In worship and meeting together we committed ourselves to the work of building bridges and strengthening relationships grounded in mutual trust. While it is never easy to put difficult history behind us, when the goal is to build up the witness of the church to the world, it can become a reality.

Jesus looked at them and said, "For mortals it is impossible, but for God all things are possible" (Matt. 19:26).

Being Part of God's Tapestry

Miriam Gross

Peple rush along gray streets lit by colorful signs. I am heading for a lunch meeting at Times Square, becoming a part of the crowd that weaves a colorful pattern of life and work into the streets of Manhattan. Tourists, like small lighthouses, stand at the center of Times Square.

Beyond all the major tourist attractions, the German Evangelical Lutheran St. Paul's Church, a congregation of the Evangelical (Lutheran) Church of Germany, is situated in the heart of the Chelsea neighborhood. Built between old brownstone houses, the church towers give a first glimpse of the building. The small, almost 175-year-old congregation serves as one of the last German-speaking Lutheran congregations in New York. Our parishioners are from the whole tri-state area (New York, New Jersey, and Connecticut), some driving up to two hours to come to church.

The members of St. Paul's are from very different walks of life. There are folk who immigrated to the United States in the 1950s or 1960s; others or their families came to New York generations ago, while expatriates and diplomats may stay only for a few years. Old and young, richer and poorer, they come here to worship God. The common bond is the German language and culture. Many refer to St. Paul's as their German home in Manhattan. Even though they all feel welcomed in this busy city, worshiping in their mother tongue seems to go deeper. With every Lord's Prayer, every Apostles' Creed said, they remember their childhood, the home they left behind, the culture of their land of origin. This is a feeling I know well.

One and a half years ago I left Germany for New York to minister to these German Lutherans in the tri-state area. It is both a privilege and a challenge. The pace of life is demanding, and the pressure on congregations is high, especially for a small traditional German congregation. Numbers are dropping because of demographic changes and the language barrier in a congregation where German is the primary language. Many German transplants have adapted easily to the American environment, often leaving behind their own traditions. In addition, speaking mostly German makes it difficult to integrate and minister to non-German spouses who speak a different language. As a result, many bilingual families become part of local

Pastor Miriam Gross in front of Deutsche Evangelisch-Lutherische St. Pauls Kirche (German Evangelical-Lutheran St. Paul's Church) in New York City. The inscription above the door is John 14:6, "I am the Way and the Truth and the Life."

English-speaking congregations. The membership of the congregation generates only a small income; this reality, combined with a long-needed refurbishment of the church building, sets St. Paul's under huge financial pressure, putting its continued existence at risk.

> "
> *Old and young, richer and poorer, they come here to worship God.*
> "

Brought up in rural Franconia, near Neuendettelsau, I had the advantage of being deeply rooted into a Lutheran surrounding. My mother, a German Lutheran, fell in love with my stepfather, a Vietnam veteran, while he was stationed in Bavaria after the war. Living in a bi-denominational family, I was introduced to ecumenism on a very personal level at a young age.

After studying in Neuendettelsau, Frankfurt, and Erlangen, I was called to a small Lutheran congregation near Rothenburg ob der Tauber. Then, being interested in ecumenism, I became part of an ecumenical project between the Evangelical Lutheran Church in Bavaria and the Church of Scotland, taking a three-year call in Orkney. This was the island from which my step-father's family had emigrated in 1860 during the potato famine, heading for the "New World" to survive and make a future for their children. When I received the call to that remote island congregation the challenges were unknown and totally unexpected: the sale of three church buildings and the unification of two separate congregations were obstacles to overcome. Seeing God's people pulling together because they were united through the one faith became a moving experience for me in ministry. And there in Orkney, with the birth of our fourth child, life came full circle, enabling a new Orcadian to be part of our family.

Returning to Bavaria, I faced very different challenges: I was the executive pastor for a large city congregation in Munich with 3,700 parishioners to be looked after. Working in a team ministry, I was responsible for the business management and employees within this congregation. While that number of congregants sounds huge to American and Scottish ears, it results from a passive church membership that begins with infant baptism. If you don't actively opt out of the church, you will stay a member, with the government automatically collecting an extra 8 percent of the income tax for the church. The challenges the Bavarian Church faces are similar to other Western churches. Declining membership and demographic changes force difficult decisions.

Now, in New York, these different experiences seem to come together as one, embracing both tradition and future in a huge tapestry of life God has chosen to weave. In my experience, all congregations near and far are part of this large piece of godly handiwork, integrating different colors and materials into a beautiful picture of faith.

About the Contributors

Claudia Bergmann is a Hebrew Bible scholar and an ELCA pastor who formerly served in the congregation in Luther's hometown of Eisleben, Germany. She is now the project coordinator for the research center Dynamics of Jewish Ritual Practices in Pluralistic Contexts from Antiquity to the Present at the University of Erfurt, Germany.

Karen Black holds the Rudi Inselmann Endowed Professorship in Organ at Wartburg College in Waverly, Iowa. She has performed organ recitals in the Castle Church in Wittenberg and St. George's Church in Eisenach, Germany, among other venues.

Walter C. Bouzard is professor of religion and chair of the Department of Religion and Philosophy at Wartburg College in Waverly, Iowa. He was co-recipient of a $10,000 prize from the Center for Theology and Natural Sciences for creating and teaching a course on religion and science at Wartburg.

Wanda Deifelt is professor of religion at Luther College in Decorah, Iowa. She is an ordained pastor of the Lutheran Church in Brazil and a member of the Bilateral Roman Catholic–Lutheran Dialogue appointed by the Lutheran World Federation.

R. Guy Erwin is bishop of the ELCA's Southwest California Synod. He previously held the Gerhard and Olga J. Belgum Chair in Lutheran Confessional Theology at California Lutheran University in Thousand Oaks, California.

Mark Granquist is associate professor of church history at Luther Seminary, St. Paul, Minnesota. He is the author of *Lutherans in America: A New History* (Fortress Press, 2015).

Miriam Gross is a pastor of German Lutheran St. Paul's Church in New York City. She previously served in Rothenburg ob der Tauber (Evangelical Lutheran Church in Bavaria), Germany; East Mainland (Church of Scotland), Orkney; and Munich (Evangelical Lutheran Church in Bavaria), Germany.

Jessica Nipp Hacker is an ELCA diaconal minister and lives out her calling as a professional fundraiser for Lutheran organizations. She has served at the ELCA's Wittenberg Center at the Lutheran School of Theology at Chicago, with the ELCA Malaria Campaign, and is now director of donor relations and donor stewardship for the ELCA.

Sarah Herzer has served, together with her husband, Thomas Herzer, as director of music ministry at the Castle Church in Wittenberg, Germany, since 2003. She is also a member of the faculty at the Evangelical Seminary in Wittenberg.

Paulina Ewa Hławiczka, a native of Poland, serves as a pastor in the Lutheran Church in Great Britain. She is also a classically trained soprano.

Elizabeth Hunter is editor of *Gather*, the magazine of Women of the ELCA. She previously served as editor of *The Little Lutheran* and *The Little Christian* and was an associate editor for *The Lutheran*.

Kathryn Johnson is director for ecumenical and inter-religious relations in the Office of Presiding Bishop of the ELCA. From 2007 to 2011, she was assistant general secretary for ecumenical affairs at the LWF Communion Office in Geneva. She also for many years taught historical theology at Louisville Presbyterian Theological Seminary.

Kathryn A. Kleinhans holds the Mike and Marge McCoy Family Distinguished Chair in Lutheran Heritage and Mission at Wartburg College in Waverly, Iowa. She also serves as lead instructor for the ELCA's International Women's Seminars in Wittenberg, Germany.

Robert Kolb is missions professor of systematic theology emeritus at Concordia Seminary, St. Louis, Missouri. He is the author of *Martin Luther and the Enduring Word of God* (2016) and co-editor of *The Oxford Handbook of Martin Luther's Theology* (with Irene Dingel and L'ubomir Batka) (2014) and of *The Book of Concord* (with Timothy J. Wengert) (2000).

About the Contributors

L. DeAne Lagerquist, professor of religion at St. Olaf College, is a historian of Christianity with particular interest in American religion, Lutheranism, and gender. She is the author of *From Our Mothers' Arms: A History of Women in American Lutheranism* and *The Lutherans*.

Nancy Larson currently serves as interim senior pastor of Redeemer Lutheran Church in Waverly, Iowa. She served the ELCA Northeastern Iowa Synod as assistant to the bishop from 2001 until 2008 and as the synod's director for evangelical mission from 2008 until 2013.

Carter Lindberg is professor emeritus of church history, Boston University School of Theology, and author of *The European Reformations* (2nd ed., Oxford: Wiley-Blackwell, 2010).

Kathryn Lohre is assistant to the presiding bishop and executive for ecumenical and inter-religious relations. From 2012 to 2013 she served as the president of the National Council of Churches, the first Lutheran and youngest woman to do so.

Martin Lohrmann is assistant professor of Lutheran confessions and heritage at Wartburg Seminary in Dubuque, Iowa. He has served congregations in Philadelphia and Ohio and is the author of *Book of Harmony: Spirit and Service in the Lutheran Confessions* (Fortress Press, 2016).

Susan Wilds McArver is professor of church history and educational ministry at Lutheran Theological Southern Seminary in Columbia, South Carolina. She has written extensively on the history of Lutheranism in the Southeast and on the history of the diaconate in North America.

Heidi Michelsen worked with the Lutheran Church of El Salvador in 1989 and again 1992–97. A deaconess, she now lives in Heredia, Costa Rica, where she directs the study abroad program for Valparaiso University, Valparaiso, Indiana, as well as short-term study trips for Augustana College, Rock Island, Illinois, and several other universities.

Scott A. Moore is completing a doctoral degree in liturgical studies at the University of Erfurt, Germany, writing about liturgies of baptismal remembrance. In addition, he leads weekly evening prayer in English at the Augustinian Monastery Church in Erfurt. He served as pastor of Saints Peter and Paul and St. Andreas in Lutherstadt Eisleben from 2003 to 2009.

Nelavala Gnana Prasuna serves as academic dean of Mennonite Brethren Centenary Bible College in Telangana, South India, and is pastor of Satyavedu Parish in the South Andhra Lutheran Church. She previously served as principal of Indian Theological Seminary and as Asia regional officer for the Lutheran World Federation.

Craig L. Nessan is academic dean and professor of contextual theology and ethics at Wartburg Theological Seminary in Dubuque, Iowa. His teaching and research include focus on reclaiming and reinterpreting the theology of the Lutheran Reformation for the life and mission of the church today.

Nicole Newman is a poet and community organizer who lives in Washington, D.C. She is a member of Luther Place Memorial Church and enjoys sunflowers, books, and chocolate.

Stanley N. Olson retired in 2014 as president of Wartburg Theological Seminary. Previously he served as the ELCA's executive director for vocation and education, as bishop of the Southwestern Minnesota Synod, as parish pastor, and as a professor at Luther Seminary, St. Paul, Minnesota.

Elizabeth Palmer serves as books editor of *The Christian Century* magazine. She is an ELCA pastor and holds a Ph.D. in theology from the University of Chicago Divinity School.

Winston D. Persaud is professor of systematic theology, director of the Center for Global Theologies, and holder of the Kent S. Knutson and United Evangelical Lutheran Church Chair in Theology and Mission at Wartburg Theological Seminary, Dubuque, Iowa.

Mitri Raheb is the pastor of the Evangelical Lutheran Christmas Church in Bethlehem (Evangelical Lutheran Church in Jordan and the Holy Land) and founder and president of the Diyar Consortium, a group of Lutheran-based, ecumenically oriented institutions serving the Bethlehem area.

Edward H. Schroeder served as professor of systematic theology at Christ Seminary–Seminex, St. Louis, Missouri. He is co-founder of the Crossings Community, a theological education network dedicated to "crossing" the scriptures and daily life.

Gary M. Simpson holds the Northwestern Lutheran Theological Seminary Chair in Theology at Luther Seminary in St. Paul, Minnesota. He is the author of *Critical Social Theory: Prophetic Reason, Civil Society, and Christian Imagination* (Fortress Press, 2001) and *War, Peace, and God: Rethinking the Just-War Tradition* (Fortress Press, 2007).

Albert Starr Jr. is director for ethnic specific and multicultural ministries and program director for African Descent Ministries in the ELCA's church-wide offices in Chicago.

Kirsi Stjerna is First Lutheran, Los Angeles / Southwest Synod Professor of Lutheran History and Theology Chair at Pacific Lutheran Theological Seminary, Berkeley, California, a graduate school of California Lutheran University. A native of Finland, she is also a docent at Helsinki University.

Kevin L. Strickland serves as assistant to the presiding bishop/executive for worship of the Evangelical Lutheran Church in America.

Alicia Vargas is associate professor of multicultural and contextual studies and dean for academic affairs at Pacific Lutheran Theological Seminary, a graduate school of California Lutheran University, in the Graduate Theological Union, Berkeley, California. She is the author of *Como estudiar la Biblia / How to Study the Bible* (Augsburg Fortress, 2009).

Kristin J. Wendland is pastor at St. Paul's Lutheran Church in Wilton, Wisconsin, and Ph.D. candidate in Old Testament at Princeton Theological Seminary.

Timothy J. Wengert is the emeritus Ministerium of Pennsylvania Professor of Church History at the Lutheran Theological Seminary at Philadelphia. A parish pastor for seven years, he is the author of many books and articles on the Reformation, including translating and editing *Martin Luther's Ninety-Five Theses* for Fortress Press in 2015.

Acknowledgments

"It's All About Grace," by Kathryn A. Kleinhans, was first published in *The Lutheran* magazine in November 2007 and is reprinted here by permission of the author.

"Lutheranism 101," by Kathryn A. Kleinhans, was first published in *The Lutheran* magazine in June 2006 and is reprinted here by permission of the author.

"Lutheranism 202," by Kathryn A. Kleinhans, was first published in *The Lutheran* magazine in October 2008 and is reprinted here by permission of the author.

"Read the Bible with Martin Luther," by R. Guy Erwin, was first published in *The Lutheran* magazine in October 2005 and is reprinted here by permission of the author.

"Discipleship and Spirituality According to Luther's Catechisms," by Edward H. Schroeder, was first published by the Crossings Community on October 13, 2005, in the Thursday Theology e-newsletter, and at www.crossings.org, and is reprinted here by permission of the author.

"Why Lutherans Care for Creation: A Profile" was first published on www.lutheransrestoringcreation.org and is reprinted here by permission of Lutherans Restoring Creation Director David Rhoads.

"'No longer Jew or Greek': Multiculturalism Has Pauline Roots," by Alicia Vargas, was first published in *The Lutheran* magazine in July 2009 and is reprinted here by permission of the author.

"I Am a Palestinian Christian," by Mitri Raheb, is excerpted from *I Am a Palestinian Christian* (Minneapolis: Augsburg Fortress, 1995) and is reprinted here by permission of Fortress Press.

Acknowledgments

IMAGE CREDITS

Page 13: Nordisk familjebok (1904). Page 14: Theses door. Castle Church, Wittenberg, Germany. Photo by User: Fewskulchor (https://de.wikipedia. org/wiki/Benutzer:Fewskulchor) / CC-BY SA-3.0 (http://creativecommons. org/licenses/by-sa/3.0/). Page 20: Painting above Theses door. Artist unknown. Wittenberg, Germany. Photo by Kathryn A. Kleinhans. Page 23: Photo by Kathryn A. Kleinhans. Page 27: Photo by Leslie Seaton (https:// creativecommons.org/licenses/by/2.0/deed.en). Page 29: Photo by Bethany Lutheran Church, Crystal Lake, Illinois. Used by permission. Page 31: Photo by Federal Emergency Management Agency. Page 33: "Luther Discovers the Bible" by Ferdinand Pauwels (1830–1904). Photo by Kathryn A. Kleinhans. Page 41: *The Small Catechism of Martin Luther*, 1529 title page. Page 51: Plaque at the Heylshof Garden in Worms, Germany. Photo by Kathryn A. Kleinhans. Page 56: Bust of Katharina von Bora Luther by Irmeltraut Appel-Bregler. Torgau, Germany. Photo by Kathryn A. Kleinhans. Page 57: "Katharina von Bora" by Nina Koch Winkel (1905-1990). Wittenberg, Germany. Photo by Kathryn A. Kleinhans. Page 60: Statue of Philip Melanchthon by Frederick Drake (1805–1882). Wittenberg, Germany. Photo by Kathryn A. Kleinhans. Page 63: Bust of Johannes Bugenhagen by Gerhard Janensch (1860-1933). Wittenberg, Germany. Photo by Torsten Schleese / CC-BY SA-3.0 (http://creativecommons.org/licenses/by-sa/3.0/). Page 66: Photo by Kathryn A. Kleinhans. Page 73: Henry Melchior Muhlenberg monument by J. Otto Schweizer (1863-1955). Philadelphia, Pennsylvania. Photo by User: Concord (https://commons.wikimedia.org/wiki/User:Concord) / CC-BY SA-3.0 (http://creativecommons.org/licenses/by-sa/3.0/) / GFDL (https:// commons.wikimedia.org/wiki/Commons:GNU_Free_Documentation_ License). Page 79: Photo by Kathryn A. Kleinhans. Page 80: Bust of Dietrich Bonhoeffer by Svirnelsis Kestutis (1976-). "Jesus in the Dungeon" chapel, Flossenbürg, Germany. Photo by Kathryn A. Kleinhans. Page 82: Photo by User: César (https://commons.wikimedia.org/wiki/User:C%C3%A9sar) / (https://creativecommons.org/licenses/by/3.0/deed.en). Page 88: Church Year frontispiece by Nicholas T. Markell, Markell Studios, Inc., in *Evangelical Lutheran Worship* (Evangelical Lutheran Church in America, admin. Augsburg Fortress, 2006), 11. Page 90: Illustration from *The Sunday Assembly* by Lorraine S. Brugh and Gordon W. Lathrop (Augsburg Fortress, 2008), 229. Page 93: Photo by Manuela Richter. Used by permission. Page 96: *The*

Eucharist © Daniel Bonnell, www.BonnellArt.com. Page 102: Photo by Kathryn A. Kleinhans. Page 105: "St. Matthew's Passion" by Johann Sebastian Bach (1685-1750). Page 110: Altarpiece by Lucas Cranach the Elder (1472–1553). Church of St. Mary, Wittenberg, Germany. Photo by David Herwaldt. Used by permission. Page 115: Photo by Kathryn A. Kleinhans. Page 125: Photo by Jessica Nipp Hacker. Used by permission. Page 150: Dance of Stained Glass © iStock/Thinkstock. Page 158: Photo by Kathryn A. Kleinhans. Page 179: Photo by Raphaël Thiémard / CC-BY-SA-2.0 (https://creativecommons.org/licenses/by-sa/2.0/deed.en). Page 185: Photo by Kristin J. Wendland. Used by permission. Page 186: Photo by Kristin J. Wendland. Used by permission. Page 192: Photo by Alan R. Schulz. Used by permission. Page 196: Photo by Kathryn A. Kleinhans. Page 203: Photo by Herbert Gross. Used by permission.